INTRODUCT

We hope that this revised edition ᴏ. ᴏᴉɡᴉɪꜱ ꜰor Beginners will provide a basic sign vocabulary for all those learning to communicate with deaf people, in particular the families of young deaf children.

We hope that it might also be appropriate to teachers and speech therapists working with pupils with severe learning difficulties and/or specific speech and language impairments, who will depend upon a signed supplement for their communication development.

522 signs are presented, together with the finger-spelling alphabet. Finger-spelling can be used to initial or spell out words, and is particularly useful for names.

Regular attendance at a signing class is recommended as the best way to learn and to clarify any regional variations of sign. A more comprehensive reference of sign can be found in our publication 'Communication Link - Third Edition'.

When communicating with a child, try to ensure that she/he is watching you, and can see your face for visual information. Try to use these signs as you talk. It is difficult at first, but it becomes easier with practice.

Speak clearly, and do not over-mouth your words, but do use plenty of facial and bodily expression. If you have difficulty understanding what a child is saying DON'T GIVE UP, DO PERSIST, the meaning may become clear.

Finally, encourage children to speak to you and each other, some may have an ability to communicate verbally and this needs to be developed.

GUIDE TO CAPTIONS

In this book, signs and finger-spelling are described and drawn as if the person making them is right handed. Naturally, left handed people will sign and finger-spell using the left hand as the dominant hand.

The captions are intended to add extra information to explain the movement of the hands which cannot always be shown in a drawing. Where possible, a full description of the sign is given, but in some cases the hand shapes may not be given if they are clear from the drawing.

To avoid misunderstandings, and lengthy descriptions, we have used set terms to describe:

1.   Parts of the hand
2.   Common hand shapes
3.   Directions

PARTS OF THE HAND

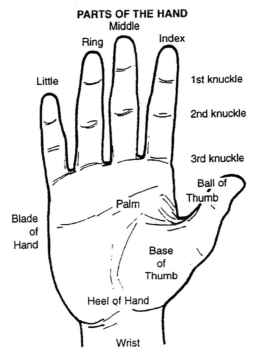

The right hand is always written as R.
The left hand is always written as L.

BASIC HAND SHAPES

Flat Hand	Open Hand	Clawed Hand	Fist

Closed Hand	Bent Hand	Bunched Hand	"O" Hand

Cupped Hand	Full "O" Hand	"Y" Hand	"L" Hand

Hand shapes based on the **Right** hand shape of British two-handed finger-spelling.

"C" Hand	Full "C" Hand	"M" Hand

"N" Hand	"R" Hand	"V" Hand

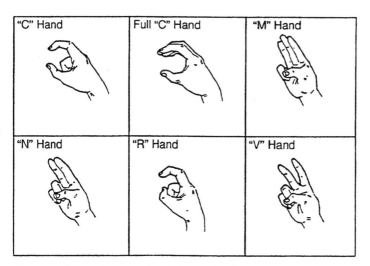

These are the most common hand shapes, but do not cover every shape used in signing. They may be further clarified, R. hand loosely cupped, L. hand slightly bent, two "v" hands, fingers bent, etc.
If the caption says, e.g. index, middle finger and thumb extended, then it is understood that the other fingers are closed.

DIRECTIONS

The terms used to describe the directions in which the hands are facing, pointing and moving are as follows:

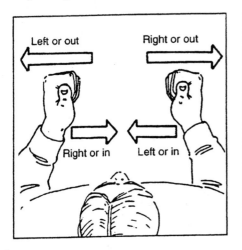
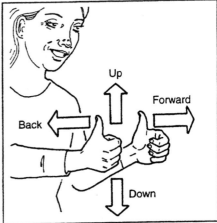

FACING
The direction the palm of the hand faces is given as "palm up", "palm back", etc. even if the hand is closed.

In the above illustrations, the R. hand is palm left, the L. hand is palm right. They may also be described as palms facing.

POINTING
The hand may be described as "pointing" up, forward, etc. even if the fingers are bent in a different direction, or closed.

In the above illustration, both hands are pointing forward, thumbs up.

MOVEMENT
Where a movement or position is diagonal, it is described as "forward/left", "back/right", etc. Many movements are described as "hands move **alternately**". This means that they move at the same time in opposite directions as in "up and down", or continuously in the same circular direction, alternately.

Some signs need a full discription of hand shapes and positions before any movement is made, this is then called a **formation**, this means they keep their position together as they move.

NUMBER SYSTEM

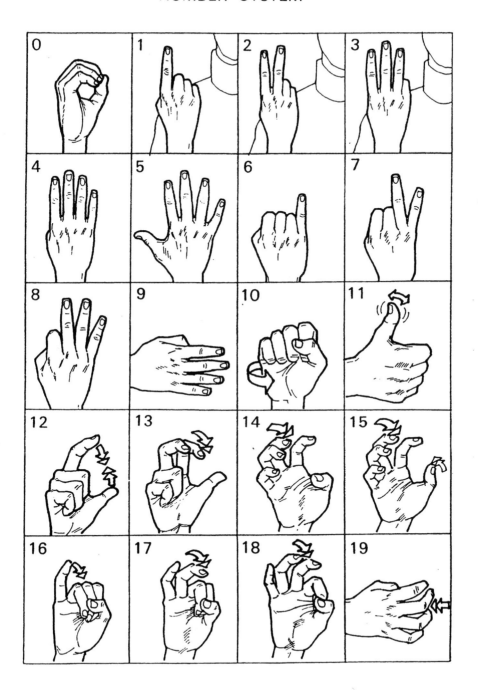

BRITISH TWO-HANDED FINGER SPELLING ALPHABET

ABOUT (approx.)

R. open hand palm down pointing forward. Hand waggles.

ABOUT (concerning)

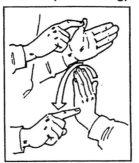

Fingerspell 'A', then sweep R. index finger over L. fingertips to spell 'T'. One of several variations.

ACCIDENT, MISHAP

Fingerspell 'A', then form letter 'C' and move R. hand away to the right in two hops. One of several variations.

ADD, EXTRA

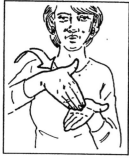

Tips of R. hand move in small arc to contact palm up L. hand in tipping movement.

ADDRESS (live)

Two flat hands, palms facing about 6" apart jerk forwards twice. One of several variations.

AEROPLANE, FLIGHT

R. closed hand, thumb and little finger extended held near head, moves forward and up.

AFTER, LATER

Extended index moves from left to right in small arc. One of several variations

AFTERNOON

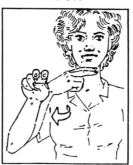

R. index and middle fingers touch chin then twist to point forward. Can brush forward against tips of L. 'N' hand.

AGAIN, REPEAT

R. 'V' hand palm left, shakes downwards twice.

1

ALL, EVERYONE

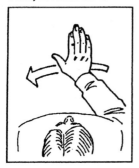

Flat hand moves in front of body in horizontal sweep.

ALWAYS, USUAL

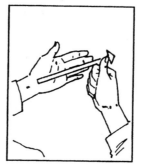

R. closed hand, thumb up, contacts heel of L. hand and sweeps along to L. fingertips. One of several variations.

AMBULANCE

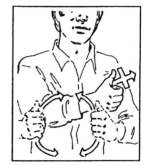

Move hands in action of steering, then draw cross on left upper arm with R. thumb. One of several variations.

AND, PLUS

R. closed hand index extended, palm up, flips over to palm down. Often fingerspelt.

ANGRY, MAD, TEMPER

Clawed hands move sharply up body twisting to palm up. Can be alternate movement. One hand may be used. Face/body indicate intensity.

ANIMAL, CREATURE

Palm down clawed hands make alternate forward circular clawing movements.

ANOTHER, OTHER

L. open hand fingers up; flick back of middle fingertip with R. index twice.

ANSWER, REPLY

Tip of R. index makes repeated contact with L. thumb tip in backward brushing movement.

ANY, WHICHEVER

R. closed hand, thumb and little finger extended, sweeps from left to right in front of body whilst waggling.

2

APPLE, FRUIT

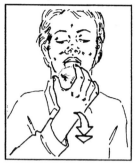

Palm back 'C' hand twists sharply from wrist to palm up near mouth twice. Handshape may vary.

ARGUE, ROW

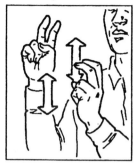

Index and middle fingers open and bent, face each other and move alternately up and down. One of several variations.

ASK, REQUEST

R. 'O' hand palm forward moves forward from side of mouth in small arc. Directional.

AUTUMN

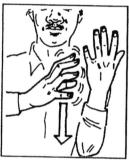

R. hand moves down from L. fingers fluttering, palm down, to indicate leaves falling.

AWAY, ABSENT

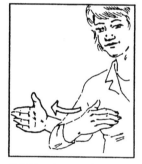

R. flat hand sweeps forward/ out.

BABY, INFANT, DOLL

Arms move from side to side in rocking movement.

BACKWARD/S

Flat hands held slightly forward, move backwards or in direction to suit context. Can be one hand only.

BAD, TERRIBLE

Little finger held up with small movement (can be forward, back or side to side). Face and body indicate negative form.

BAG, CARRIER

Closed hand held in action of holding a bag with slight up and down movement to suit context.

3

BAKED BEANS

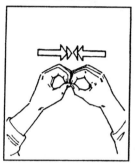

Tips of fingers in fingerspelt 'B' formation tap together twice.

BALL, GLOBE

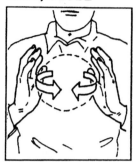

Fingers of both hands open and curved, swivel round to indicate shape and size of ball/sphere.

BALLOON, INFLATE

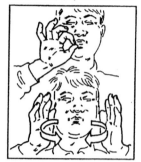

Tips of 'O' hand contact lips, then open hands move apart in outline of balloon.

BANANA

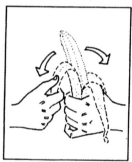

Hands move in action of holding and peeling banana. Can be outline of shape with thumbs and index fingers.

BANDAGE, HOSPITAL

R. hand moves in action of holding and winding bandage, around L. hand, or to suit context. Can be two flat hands (Hospital).

BAT, BATTING

Hand moves in action of holding and striking with a bat, appropriate to context.

BATH, BATHING

Hands move up and down several times in contact with the chest. Flat hands can be used.

BEAR, GRIZZLY

Clawed hands held in front of body move alternately from shoulders with fierce expression.

BEAUTIFUL, SUPERB

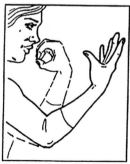

Full 'O' hand contacts lips and moves forward, springing open.

BECAUSE

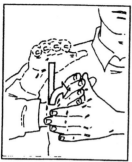

L. flat hand held with thumb up. R. flat hand contacts edge of L. index, then inside of L. thumb.

BED, SLEEP

Rest head against palm-together hands. One hand may be used.

BEEFBURGER

Full 'C' hands held near mouth. One hand may be used. Can be palm-together clawed hands, R. on L. reverse to L on R.

BEFORE, PRIOR

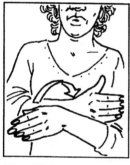

Edge of R. flat hand moves up left forearm in small arc. One of several variations.

BEFORE, PAST

R. hand makes repeated backward movement near right shoulder.

BEHAVE!

R. extended index makes short forward movement, then changes to flat hand brushing down body.

BELL, RING

R. open hand palm back shakes from side to side from wrist. Can be forward pushing movement by thumb.

BELT

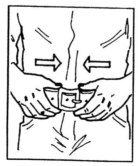

Indicate outline of belt at waist.

BEST

R. thumb strikes tip of L. thumb once in forward movement.

5

BETTER

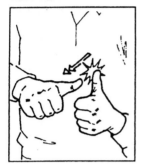

R. thumb strikes tip of L. thumb twice in a forward movement.

BETWEEN

Blade of flat R. hand waggles between middle and index finger of L. hand.

BICYCLE, BIKE

Fists make alternate forward circles in action of cycling. Handshapes may vary.

BIG, LARGE

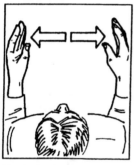

Hands move apart with emphasis. Sign varies in context.

BIRD, BEAK

Index finger and thumb open and close in front of mouth like a beak.

BIRTHDAY

Blades of flat hands on either sides of waist move forward /in then up and sweep apart.

BISCUIT

Fingertips of R. clawed hand tap near left elbow twice.

BLACK (person)

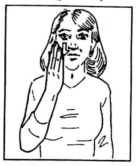

Flat hand makes small movement down cheek. Closed hand may be used.

BLANKET, COVERS

Closed hands move simultaneously up body.

6

BLIND (person)

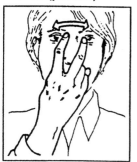

'V' hand with fingers slightly bent move from side to side in front of eyes. Can be 'N' hand moving across the eyes.

BLOOD, BLEED/ING

Two open hands pointing forward, R. on top of L.; R. hand moves forward/down off L.

BLOUSE

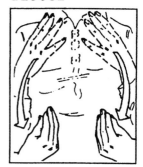

Hands move down body, closing to bunched hands to indicate the shape of a blouse.

BLUE

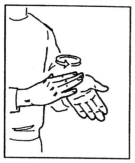

R. flat hand makes small circular movement on L. palm or wrist. Can be made on back of palm down L. hand.

BOAT, FERRY, SAIL

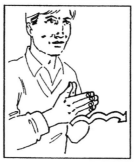

Tips of fingers touching, hands at an angle, move forward bobbing up and down.

BODY, WEAR

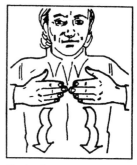

Flat hands move down the body. One hand may be used.

BOIL, BUBBLE

Indexes point up and move in alternate small upward circles, like bubbles rising.

BOOK, CATALOGUE

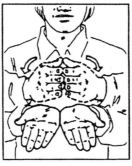

Two flat hands pointing forward, palm to palm, open to palms up.

BOTTLE, TIN

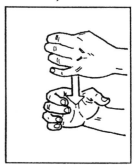

Two full 'C' hands, L. above R.; R. hand moves down. Can be R. above L. and R. hand moves up.

7

BOWL, BASIN, SINK

Indicate shape of bowl using cupped hands, blades together curving apart.

BOX

Flat hands palms back, L. in front of R. move to palms facing indicating sides of box.

BOY

R. index brushes left across chin. Can be index and thumb stroking down chin, or tips of 'N' hand brushing down chin. Regional.

BREAD, SLICE

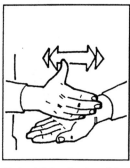

Blade of R. hand makes slicing action on L. palm. One of several variations.

BREAK, SNAP

Fists held together, palm down, twist apart in snapping action.

BREAKFAST

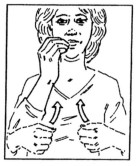

Closed hands move up body several inches from waist, then bunched hand moves to mouth. Regional.

BRIGHT, CLEAR

Hands move sharply upwards and apart, springing open from full 'O' hands. Directional.

BRING, FETCH

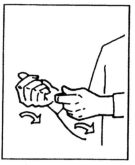

R. hand in front of L., pull hands back/left in small arc to body closing to fists. Directional.

BROTHER

Two closed hands, thumbs up, rub together at 2nd knuckles.

8

BROWN

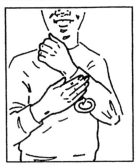

R. flat hand makes small anti-clockwise circle on left arm. One of several regional signs.

BRUSH (hairbrush)

Hand moves in action of using a hair brush.

BUILD, BUILDING

Flat hands alternate R. above L. then L above R. brushing against each other as they move upwards.

BUS, MINIBUS

Hands (can be palm up) make steering movement; thumb makes small forward movement (can be bent 'V' hand). Regional

BUSY, HARD WORK

Blade of R. flat hand swivels forward/down over edge of L. Can be repeated. The cheeks may be puffed.

BUT

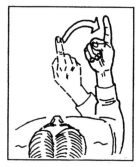

R. index extended and pointing forward palm down. Twist over to palm up. Often fingerspelt.

BUTTER, SPREAD

Edge of R. 'N' hand makes small repeated scraping movement on L. palm.

BUTTERFLY

Flat hands palms back, wrists crossed thumbs locked. Bend and straighten fingers a few times like wings.

BUY, PURCHASE

Thumb tucked into bent R. index, move in forward arc from L. palm. One of several variations.

9

CABBAGE

L. fist palm back; make chopping action with R. flat hand on knuckle edge of L. fist.

CAKE, SCONE

Tips of R. clawed hand tap back of L. hand. Movement can be repeated.

CAN, ABLE

'C' hand pointing back in front of nose moves forward/down as index flexes. Can be located on the forehead.

CAN'T, UNABLE

Index moves down and loops over in the form of an X, accompanied by head shake. May start from forehead.

CAR, DRIVE

Closed hands in action of holding and moving steering wheel. (Extended fingers of palm in 'O' hands flex, NE regional).

CAREFUL/LY

Indexes held under eyes; index fingers flex as hands move forward/down.

CARPET, FLOOR

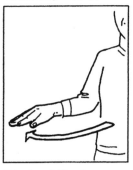

Palm down flat hand sweeps across horizontally. Can be both hands moving apart.

CARROT

R. fist, palm forward twists at side of mouth as if taking a bite.

CARRY, PASS ON

Bent hands move in carrying action. Will vary in context.

CAT

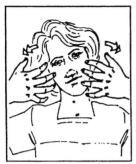

Fingers flex as hands move out from sides of mouth to indicate whiskers. Can be R. hand stroking back of L. closed hand

CAULIFLOWER

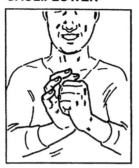

Place L. fist into loosely cupped R. hand. Regional.

CHAIR, SEAT, SIT

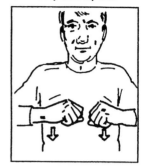

Closed hands move down slightly with stress. Can be fingers of R. bent 'V' hand hooking over L. index.

CHANGE, ALTER

Indexes extended with hands facing and in contact, twist to change positions. One of a number of variations.

CHANGE (cash)

R. flat hand contacts L., then makes backward circle around L. and contacts again.

CHEESE

Tips of R. bent hand touch L. palm as hand rocks slightly forward/back or side to side in indication of wedge.

CHEW

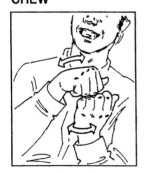

Two closed hands, R. o on top of L. make small circular rubbing movement against each other.

CHICKEN

Index finger and thumb open and close as elbow move in and out.

CHILDREN

Palm down flat hand makes small downward repeated movement a few inches apart. Two hands may be used.

11

CHIPS

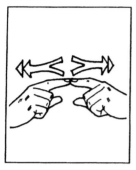

Index fingers and thumbs form outline of chips in repeated movement. One of several variations.

CHOCOLATE

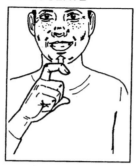

Index edge of R. 'C' hand taps against the chin twice. One of several regional signs.

CHOOSE, SELECT

Index closes onto thumb as hand moves backwards. Both hands ban be used alternately. Directional.

CHRISTMAS, SANTA

Fingers and thumb hold and stroke down the chin as fingers close onto the thumb.

CHURCH, CHAPEL

R. fist on top of L., hands make short repeated movement up and down.

CINEMA, PICTURES

Heel of R. open hand palm forward rests on L. index and shakes from side to side.

CLASS/ROOM

'C' hands touch at fingertips then swivel in forward arc to finish with blades touching. One of several variations.

CLEAN, CLEAR

R. flat hand sweeps forward along palm up L. hand.

CLEVER, BRIGHT

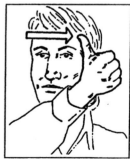

Thumb tip moves across forehead in sharp movement.

CLIMB/ER, CLIMBING

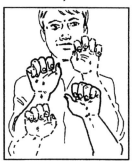

Palm forward clawed hands make upward climbing movements alternately. Will vary in context.

CLOCK, TIME

R. thumbtip contacts centre of L. palm as extended index 'ticks' round. May be just R. index moving in smooth movement.

CLOSE (door)

R. flat hand swivels from palm left to palm back against back of L. flat hand. Will vary to suit context.

CLOTHES, CLOTHING

Hands brush down the body twice.

COAT, JACKET

Hands move in action of pulling a coat/jacket over shoulders.

COFFEE

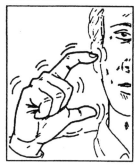

'C' hand makes small quick twisting movements near mouth. Can be R. fist on top of L. making grinding movement.

COLD, CHILLY

Closed hands held close together in front of chest; elbows pull into body in shivering action.

COLD, FLU, HANKY

Hand moves in repeated action of using hanky.

COLOUR

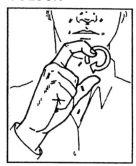

R. 'C' hand palm left makes small vertical circles in front of chin. One of several variations.

13

COME

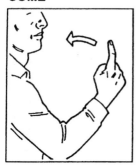

R. extended index, held away from body, moves back towards body. Index may be curved.

CONTINUE, CARRY ON

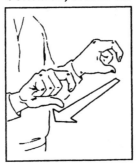

Two 'C' hands move from left to right, or forward together simultaneously.

COOK, PAN

Hand makes short repeated movement backwards and forwards. One of several variations.

COOKER

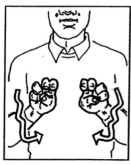

'N' hands pointing forward move down with quick twisting movement. 'V' hands can be used. Regional.

COOKERY, WHISK

Left arm held bent. R. hand moves in whisking action.

COOL, AIR

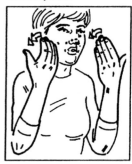

Fingers make several short backward bending movements near cheeks.

CORNFLAKES, CEREAL

Hands move in action of holding and shaking a cereal packet.

COUGH

Index edge of fist thumps twice against chest.

COUNT, ADD UP

Hand moves up with fingers wiggling. Fingers can point in. Both hands can be used.

COUNTRYSIDE

R. hand starts at L. fingertips and sweeps forward and left up left arm. One of several variations.

COW

Thumbs and little fingers extended; thumbs on temples, twist from palm down to palm forward. One hand may be used.

CRASH, HIT

R. fist hits L. palm. Can be two fist banging together, or similar to suit context.

CRY, TEARS

Index moves down cheek several times. Both hands may be used. Sign varies in context.

CUCUMBER

Whole L. 'C' hand palm down; R. flat hand makes slicing movement against L. One of several variations.

CULTURE

R. hand closes onto L. palm, then moves forward slightly twisting to palm forward.

CUPBOARD

Hands move in action of opening doors appropriate to context.

CUSTARD, SAUCE

'Y' hand with thumb pointing down moves in horizontal circle. Regional.

CUT, CUT BACK/OFF

'V' hand makes short forward movement as fingers snap shut. Fingers may brush past tip of L. index pointing right.

15

CUTLERY, MEAL

Two 'N' hands, fingers of R. resting on top of L. at right angles make small sawing action.

DANCE, DANCING

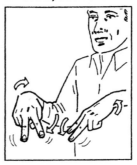

'V' hands make downward flicking movements from wrists as hands move from side to side. 'N' hands may be used.

DAY, LIGHT

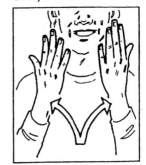

Palm back flat hands start crossed and swing upwards and apart from the elbows. *Day* is often fingerspelt.

DEAD, DEATH, DIE

Palm facing 'N' hands twist down sharply from wrists to point forward. If movement is slow, the meaning is *dying*.

DEAF, DEAF PERSON

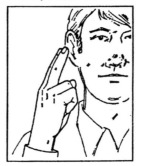

Tips of 'N' hand contact ear.

DIFFERENT

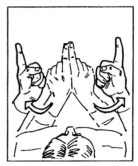

Indexes held together, palm down, move apart twisting to palm up.

DINNER, MEAL

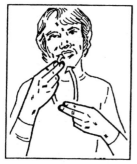

Palm back 'N' hands move alternately up to mouth. Can be two 'N' hands edge to edge making small sawing movement.

DIRT/Y, GRIMY

Palms of open hands rub from side to side against each other (can be circular movement), with appropriate facial expression.

DO

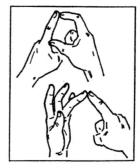

Fingerspell 'D' 'O'. Can be R. fist striking top of L. or other forms depending on context.

16

DOCTOR

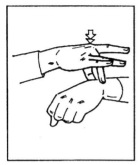

R. middle finger and thumb tips tap L. wrist twice. Index and thumb tips can be used.

DOG

'N' hands pointing down make small movements down. Also back of bent hand under chin, or flat hand tapping thigh, (regional).

DOLE, BENEFIT

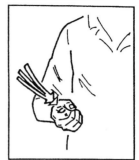

Palm up clawed hand makes repeated movement back/down into body, closing to a fist.

DON'T, DO NOT

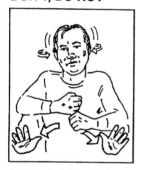

R. fist contacts top of L. then open hands start crossed and swing sharply apart. Can be second part of sign only.

DOOR, GATE

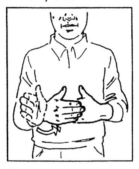

Flat hands held together, R. in front of L., R. pivots from wrist to point forward, and back again. May vary in context.

DOWN, SOUTH

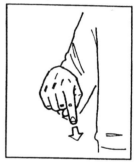

Index pointing down moves down in small movement.

DRAW, SKETCH

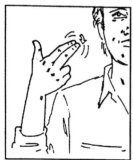

Palm back 'N' hand makes small repeated movement. Will change in context.

DRAWER/S

The hands pull back towards the body. Movement is repeated in downward position for plural.

DREAM, FANTASY

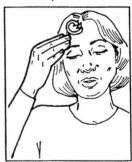

Tips of bent hand move in small circular movement near the forehead.

17

DRESS, GET DRESSED

Open hands brush down body, and slightly apart to finish palm down. A short quick repeated movement means *get dressed*.

DRINK, GLASS

Full 'C' hand moves up with small tipping movement near mouth.

DROP, LET FALL

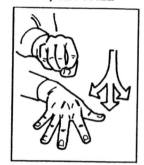

R. full 'O' hand moves down, springing open. If R. hand starts on L. palm then moves off springing open, the meaning is *omit*.

DRY, DRIED

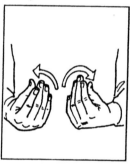

The thumbs rub across the pads of the fingers. One hand may be used.

EASTER

Tips of two clawed hands tap together twice, (regional). Can be R. index finger drawing cross on the back of L. hand.

EASY, SIMPLE, SOFT

Index finger prods the cheek twice. Cheeks may be puffed out meaning *dead easy, doddle*.

EAT, FOOD, SNACK

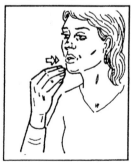

Bunched hand makes small repeated movement backwards towards mouth.

EGG

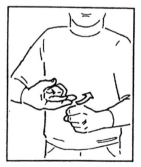

R. 'N' hand (can be bent index) makes slicing movement above L. fist. Can be bent 'V' hands touching then twisting down/apart.

ELECTRIC/ITY, BATTERY

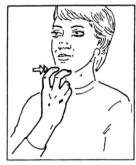

Tips of R. bent 'V' hand tap chin twice. *Electricity* can also be signed with index moving down in sharp zig-zag.

EMPTY, FLAT

R. flat hand moves down onto L. Can end with hands brushing across each other. Will vary in context.

END, FINAL, LAST

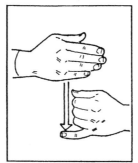

Palm back R. flat hand moves down onto extended L. little finger. R. hand can also be palm down or palm up.

ENOUGH, PLENTY, AMPLE

Backs of fingers of palm back bent hand brush upwards/forwards twice under chin.

EVERYTHING, WHOLE

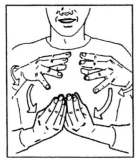

Open hands pointing in towards each other, move out and down twisting to palm up bunched hands.

FALL, FALL OVER

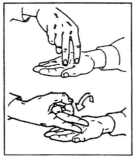

R. 'V' hand (legs classifier) stands on L. palm then twists over to palm up. Handshape and movement may change in context.

FAMILY

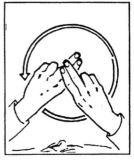

Fingerspelt 'F' formation moves in small horizontal circle. Can be palm down open hand in same movement.

FARM, FARMER

R. thumb extended, pointing left contacts upper chest then moves in forward arc to contact lower chest.

FAST, SHARP, SPEED

R. index on top of L. index; R. hand springs sharply open in backward movement. One of several variations.

FAT, OBESE, STOUT

Closed hands with thumbs extended move apart and backwards towards body. Cheeks may be puffed. May vary in context.

19

FATHER, DAD, DADDY

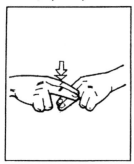

Fingers of fingerspelt 'F' formation tap together twice. Can also mean *Friday* in some regions.

FAVOURITE, PREFER/ENCE

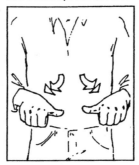

Closed hands with thumbs extended make two small downward movements. One of several variations.

FED UP, HAD ENOUGH

Bent hand moves firmly up under chin (can be repeated). Face and body show negative feeling, or can change meaning to *full*.

FEEL, EMOTION, SENSE

Tips of middle fingers brush upwards on body (open hands may be used). May be repeated. One hand may be used.

FIELD, MEADOW, GREEN

R. flat hand sweeps up the length of left forearm.

FIGHT, CONFLICT

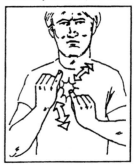

Extended little fingers bang together several times. May vary in context.

FIND, DISCOVER

Index moves down from near eye as hand moves forward then sharply up, snapping closed to a fist in a grasping movement.

FINGERSPELL, SPELL

Finger and thumb tips of bunched hands contact with fingers wiggling as formation moves right (for British two handed system).

FINISH, COMPLETE

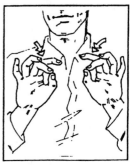

Middle fingers and thumb tips make quick repeated contact. Regional. One hand may be used. One of several variations.

FIRE, BURN, FLAMES

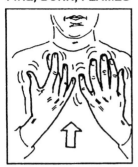

Palm back hands move upwards with fingers wiggling. Can be palm facing, moving up and down alternately. May vary in context.

FIRST, INITIAL

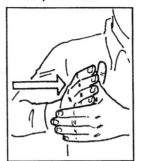

R. hand strikes inside of L. thumb. Can be palm forward index twisting sharply to palm back, or several other regional signs.

FISH, SWIM

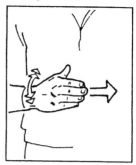

Flat hand moves forward with slight twisting movement from wrist.

FISH FINGERS

Thumb tip of open hand held on chin as fingers wiggle, then tips of index fingers and thumbs tap together twice.

FIX/ED, FIRM, STABLE

Index fingers hooked together make short, firm movement down, or forward. Also means *resolute, committed, determined.*

FIX, MEND, REPAIR

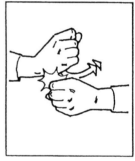

R. fist brushes across top of L. fist twice. Can be repeated contact with tips of bunched hands twisting against each other

FLOWER, GARDEN

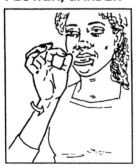

'O' hand moves from side to side under nose. A bunched hand may be used.

FOG, HAZE, MIST

Palm forward open hands move in alternate, slow circular movements in front of face, or may slowly cross over each other.

FOLLOW, GO ALONG WITH

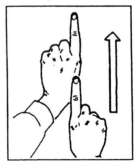

Indexes point and move forward R. behind L. Indexes can be upright (person classifiers), and also mean *work shadow.*

21

FOOD, BREAKFAST, EAT

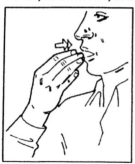

Bunched hand makes small repeated movement backwards towards mouth. Also used for other meals; *lunch, supper, tea.*

FOOTBALL/ER, SOCCER

Indexes extended and pointing down ('V' hands can be used); R. flicks forward and L. back in sharp movement. Regional.

FOREVER, ETERNAL

Index tips contact each other, then R. hand moves out to the right in spiralling movement. The cheeks may be puffed.

FORGET, FORGETFUL

Tips of full 'O' hand touch forehead then hand springs open in short forward movement. One of several variations.

FORK, TOAST

Tips of R. 'V' hand prod L. palm, movement may be repeated.

FRIEND, MATE, PAL

R. hand clasps L. in short shaking movement, or closed hands, thumbs up, bang together or twist against each other (regional).

FRIGHTENED, FEAR

Clawed hands tap chest twice. Can be one hand only. Body moves back slightly. Also means *scared, terrified.* One of several variations.

FROM, WHERE FROM?

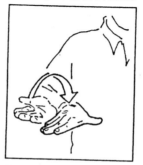

Hand flips sharply over to palm down, or palm down R. flat hand brushes down past L. palm, (also meaning *decide, about).* Face shows question form.

FRONT

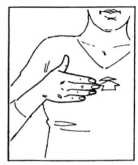

Flat hand taps front of chest twice. Will change in context. This version also means *like, fond of.*

FRUIT

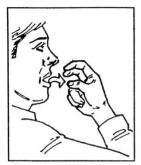

'N' hand with thumb and fingers bent makes small upwards movement near mouth. Can be repeated. Handshape may vary.

FULL, COVER

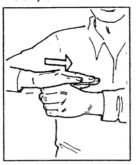

R. hand brushes across top of L. fist, (movement can be circular) or palm down flat hands; R. moves up to contact underside of L.

FUNNY, LAUGH

Bent index and thumb shake slightly from side to side near chin. Two hands can be used in altenate movement, L. under R.

FURNITURE

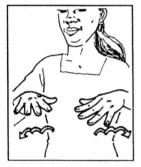

Palm down open hands make short repeated downward movements as they move apart.

GAME, PLAY

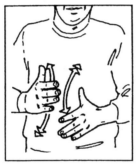

Open hands brush alternately up and down against each other twice. Can be fingerspelt 'G' formation, or other variation.

GARDEN/ER, DIG

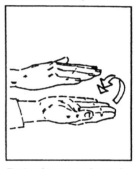

Flat hand turns over from palm up to palm down in small repeated forward movement. One of several variations.

GAS (fuel)

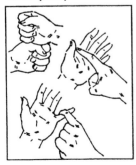

Commonly fingerspelt. For *gas, anaesthetic,* palm back clawed hand is held over face.

GET, GOT, ACHIEVE/MENT

Palm left R. clawed hand moves left closing to a fist. Also means adopt/ion. WIth sharp movement, also means *grab, snatch.*

GIRL, LASS

Index makes small strokes forward twice in cheek (or across chin). Can be index pointing left, moving to right on brow (regional)

GIVE, HAND OVER, PASS

Hands move forward together (can be one hand). Handshape and direction may change in context. Also means *gift, offer, present.*

GLASSES, OPTICIAN, SPECS

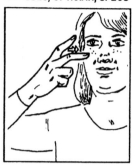

Tip of middle fingertip of 'V' hand taps upper cheek twice. Can be both hands. 'O' hands sometimes used, held in front of eyes.

GLOVE, GLOVES

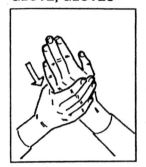

R. hand moves down in action of pulling a glove over L. hand. Repeat L. on R. for plural.

GLUE, PASTE, SPREAD

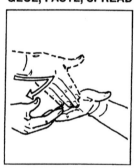

R. hand moves left, then bends and drags backs of fingers right along L. palm. Can be edge of R. fist moving/twisting on L. palm.

GO, GO AWAY, SEND

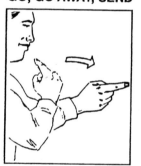

Index swings forward, pointing away from body. A flat hand can be used. Will vary in context.

GOING TO, EXPECT, INTEND

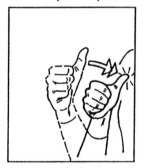

Back of extended thumb taps side of upper chest twice, with slight forward movement of body.

GOOD, GREAT, HELLO

Extended thumb makes small movement forward, both hands may be used. With raised eyebrows also means *all right?*

GOOD MORNING, MORNING

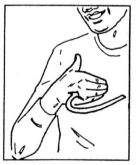

Tips of R. bent hand, thumb up, touch left, then right upper chest. Can be two bent hands, or closed hands, moving up chest (regional).

GOODBYE, BYE, CHEERIO

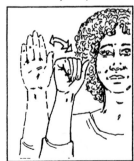

Hand bends at palm knuckles in repeated movement, or shakes slightly from side to side.

GRANDFATHER, GRANDAD

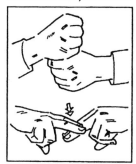

Fingerspelt 'G' followed by quick repetition of fingerspelt 'F'.

GRANDMOTHER, GRANDMA

Fingerspelt 'G' followed by quick repetition of fingerspelt 'M'.

GRASS, VEGETATION

Palm back R. hand with fingers wiggling moves along behind left forearm. One of several variations.

GREED, GREEDY, SELFISH

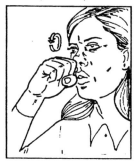

Fist moves in small circles in front of nose. Can be located on chin. Can be palm up closed hand tapping waist twice.

GREEN

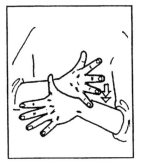

Open hands crossed at wrists tap together twice or palm down R. hand brushes up left arm, or middle finger flicks left shoulder (all regional)

GREY

Closed hands (little fingers may be extended) rub against each other in circular movement. One of several regional variations.

GROW/TH, DEVELOP, CREATE

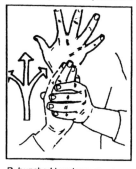

R. bunched hand moves up as fingers open, through L. full 'C' hand. For *grow, expand*, palm in open hands move apart, or other in context.

GUESS, CONCEPT

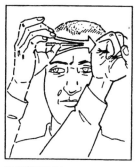

Full 'C' hand moves across forehead closing to a fist. Can be index moving forward in small loop from forehead, ('C' hand for *concept*).

HALF, PART, PARTLY

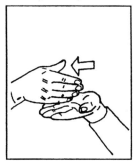

Blade down R. flat hand makes slicing movement across L. palm (sometimes made across body) Can be R. index slicing across L.

25

HANDICAP, DISABILITY

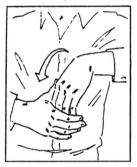

R. hand pushes L. hand fingers down/back, or extended indexes pointing down move up/down alternately (also means *limping*).

HAPPEN, CROP UP, OCCUR

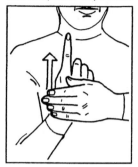

R. index moves up sharply behind L. hand, or index flicks upwards in front of L. hand (emphatically or *suddenly*).

HAPPY, ENJOY, PLEASURE

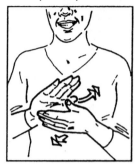

Flat hands brush against each other twice. Can be circular rubbing of flat hand on chest. Face/body show positive feeling.

HARD, HARD TO DO

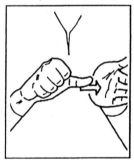

R. thumb tip prods L. palm. Repeated for *difficult problem*. With twisting movement means wood, (also *really*, regional).

HAVE, GET, POSSESS

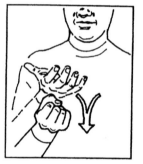

Palm up clawed hand moves down slightly, closing sharply to a fist.

HE, HER, HIM, IT, SHE

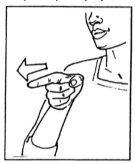

Index indicates person/thing referred to, accompanied by eye gaze. A sideways sweep indicates plural. Directional.

HEAR, LISTEN

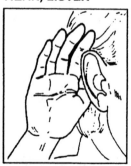

Slightly cupped hand is held behind the ear. Head may be turned slightly.

HEARING, HEARING PERSON

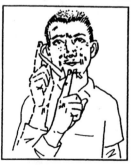

Tip of index finger contacts ear then chin (may tap chin twice). Sometimes made with extended thumb.

HEARING AID (behind the ear)

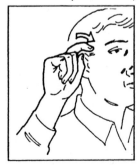

Bent index contacts side of head above ear, or twists backwards from the wrist. Will change in context for different models.

HELLO

Palm forward open hand moves to right in small arc. Hand may twist right at wrist closing to thumb up, palm left, or other variation.

HELP, AID, ASSIST

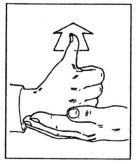

Edge of R. closed hand rest on L. palm and formation moves in direction appropriate to context (directional).

HER, HE, HIM, IT, SHE

Index indicates person/thing referred to, accompanied by eye gaze. A sideways sweep indicates plural. Directional.

HERE, THIS

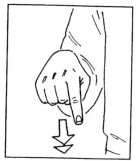

Index finger makes two short movements down (can be single movement). Both hands may be used.

HIDE, HIDDEN

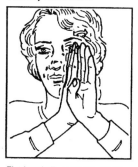

Flat hands R. behind L. make small alternate side to side movements, in front of face (in front of mouth for *secret, private*)

HOLD, HOLD ONTO, GRIP

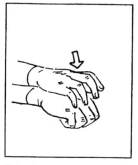

Palm down clawed hand moves down slightly closing to a fist. Will change in context.

HOLIDAY, VACATION

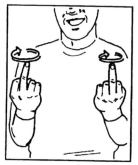

Extended middle fingers make small circular movements (handshape can be thumbs tuck into bent indexes). or other regional signs.

HOME, GO HOME, AT HOME

Bent hand palm forward twists to palm down, in forward arc, (tips of both hands touch, then move down/apart for *home, house*).

HORSE, RIDING

Fists held together move up and down. Can be one fist on top of the other, or other variations.

27

HOSPITAL, FIRST AID

R. thumb tip (can be index tip) draws small cross on left upper arm. One of many variations. Also means *ambulance, nurse*.

HOT, HEAT

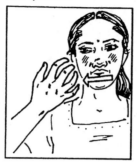

R. clawed hand moves sharply left to right in front of mouth. Can be flat hand drawn across forehead, then shaking downwards.

HOUR, HOURLY

R. 'O' hand makes forward circle on L. palm, or back of L. wrist. Can be R. index twisting in full circle on L. palm or back of wrist.

HOUSE, HOME

Tips of 'N' hands contact at an angle, then move apart/down in outline of building. Flat hands can be used.

HOW OLD? AGE, AGED

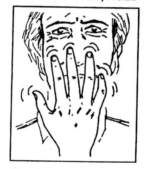

Fingers wiggle against the nose (raised eyebrows from question from). Number handshape moves forward from nose for specific age.

HUNGRY, HUNGARY

Bent hands swivel over to palm up, fingers in contact with lower chest (or closed hand rubs up/down on stomach, or other variation).

HURRY UP, QUICKLY

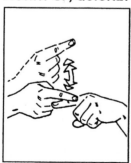

R. index taps on L. several times very quickly. With appropriate facial/bodily expression, also means *emergency, urgent*.

HURT, PAINFUL, SORE

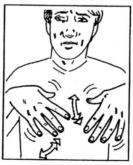

Open hands shake up and down alternately. Can be one hand. Face/body indicate negative form. Also means *injure, suffer*.

I, ME

Index fingertip touches chest.

ICECREAM

Closed hand makes two short downward movements in front of mouth. Mouth may be open with tongue slightly protruding.

IF

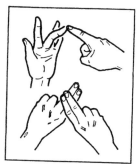

Fingerspell "IF".

IN, INTO, GO IN

R. bent hand moves forward/under L. hand, straightening to a flat hand. May vary.

INSIDE, INDOORS

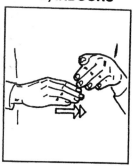

R. bent hand makes two short movements under palm down L. hand. Also means *internal*. May vary.

JUG, POUR

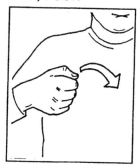

Closed hand makes bending movement from wrist in pouring action. Thumb and little finger extended gives *teapot*.

JUMPER, SWEATER

CLosed hands contact upper, then lower chest.

JUST, JUST NOW, ONLY

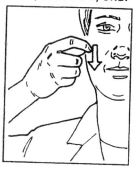

Index and thumb tip touching, hand makes short movement down cheek. An 'O' hand may be used.

KEEP, HOLD ONTO

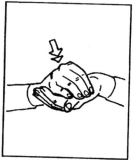

R. bent hand taps L bent hand twice. If the sign starts with index moving down from the eye, the meaning is *look after, care for*.

KEY, LOCK, UNLOCK

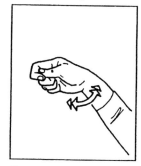

Thumb tucked into bent index, hand makes quick twisting movement from wrist. A clockwise turn gives **lock**, anti-clockwise, *unlock*.

29

KICK, KICK OUT, SACK

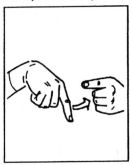

R. index pointing down swings sharply forward brushing L. index tip. Directional. Also means *dismiss, fire, suspend.*

KISS, PECK

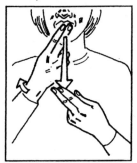

Tips of R. 'N' hand touch lips, then twist to palm down and contact tips of L. 'N' hand (will vary in context). One of several variations.

KITCHEN

Middle knuckle of R. bent index taps middle of L. extended index twice. Can be repeated contact of fingerspelt 'K'.

KNIFE, CUTLERY, MEAL

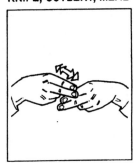

Edge of R. 'N' hand makes repeated sawing movement on edge of L. 'N' hand. Also means *dinner, restaurant, Sheffield.*

KNOW, KNOWLEDGE

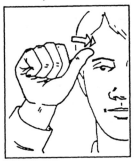

Tip of extended thumb contacts forehead twice; the head can be tilted forward slightly

DON'T KNOW

Tips of flat hand (or bent hand) on forehead, move forward/down to palm up, with head shake and corners of mouth turned down.

LATE

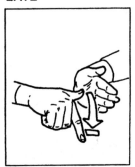

Tip of R. thumb maintains contact with L palm as hand swivel sharply forward/down. May be index only, with thumb tucked in.

LAZY, IDLE

R. hand taps left elbow twice (R. clawed hand gives *biscuit*), or palm back closed hands, middle fingers up, move down twice.

LEAD, LEADER, GUIDE

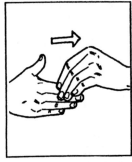

Fingers of L. hand hold R. hand fingers, moving to the left.

LEARN, ABSORB, STUDY

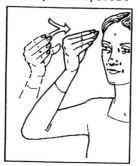

Open hand moves back to head closing to bunched hand, or index edges of R. palm down flat hands rub together, (*train, practice*).

LET, GIVE PERMISSION

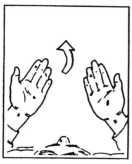

Palm up flat hands move forward together in small arc, or indexes point in and shake forward/down from wrists (*let allow*).

LIE, LIAR, FIB, UNTRUTH

Edge of R. index pointing left rubs across chin sharply to the right. Is also one version of *Russia, Russian.*

LEAVE, LEFT, DEPART

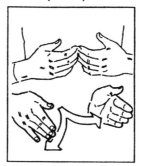

Palm back bent hands twist sharply forward and straighten. Can be one hand palm back flicking forward/away from signer.

LETTER, MAIL

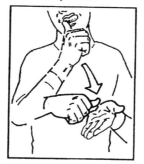

R. thumb tip touches mouth, then moves down to touch L. index. Also sometimes used to mean *stamp, insurance.*

LIGHT, DAY, DAWN

Palm back flat hands start crossed, then swing upwards and apart, (refers to *brightness, daylight,* or *light* in colour).

LEMONADE, FIZZY DRINK

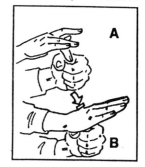

R. middle finger brushes top of L. fist. Also used as expletive with appropriate lip-pattern.

LIE, LIE DOWN

R. 'V' hand (legs classifier) lays on L. palm with short movement right. R. hand twisting palm down and back, gives toss and turn.

LIGHT, LAMP

Full 'O' hand springs open (*light on*), or closes (*light off*), located/directed appropriate to context. also means *sun, sunshine.*

31

LIKE, APPROVE, ENJOY

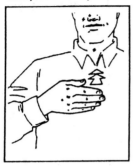

Hand taps chest twice (also means *fond of*). Open hand on chest moves forward, and closes with index up to give *if you like, please yourself*.

DON'T LIKE, DISLIKE

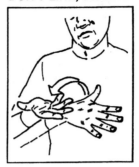

Open hand on chest twists palm up, moving forward, with negative expression, and headshake. Can be palm down, away from body.

LISTEN, TAKE IN

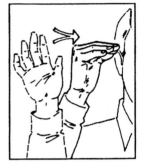

Hand moves towards ear, as fingers close onto thumb (towards eye for take in visually, or palm forward 'V' hand, fingers flexing).

LITTLE, BIT, FEW

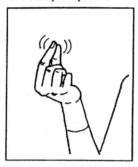

Pads of thumb and index rub together several times, or hand makes short forward/backward movement. Also means *almost, nearly*.

LONG, LONG TIME, AGES

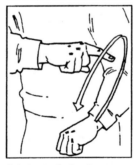

R. index (or flat hand) moves slowly up left forearm (can end by index touching back of L. wrist). Also means *slow, slowly*.

LONG TIME AGO, PAST

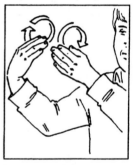

Flat hands circle backwards round each other over right shoulder (cheeks, may by puffed). Also means *history, once upon a time*.

LOOK, SEE, WATCH

"V' hand moves forward from near eye, or will be located and directed with movement appropriate to context.

LOTTERY (national lottery)

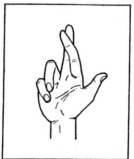

Hand is held palm forward, with index and middle fingers crossed and thumb extended.

LOUD, LOUDLY, DIN

Index makes small circle near ear and moves out as fingers crossed and thumb extended.

LOVE, AFFECTION

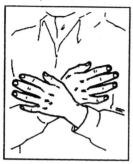

Crossed over hands on chest.
For *love, adore, fond of,* palm
back flat hands touch chest,
then closed palm down,
thumbs extended.

MAKE, CREATE, FIX

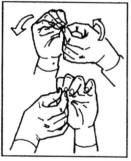

Tips of bunched hands twist
against each other, twice, (if
hands also move up, meaning
is *constructive*). Can be R. fist
striking top of L.

MANY, LOTS, HOW MANY?

Hands move apart, fingers
wiggling. Cheeks may be
puffed. Also means *too many,
too much.* Raised eyebrows for
question form.

LOVELY, DELICIOUS

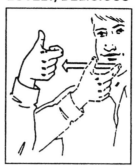

Index finger of 'L' hand
brushes across chin and curls
in. Also means *nice, sweet,
tasty.* On cheek, means *pretty,
young* (regional).

MAN, MALE, MASCULINE

Hand strokes chin as fingers
close onto thumb, may be
repeated, or palm left R. full 'C'
hand moves forward from chin
closing to a fist.

MATTER, WRONG

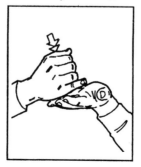

Edge of R. little finger taps L.
palm twice. Also means *evil,
fault, sin.* Eyebrows raised for
*what's the matter?, what's
wrong?*

LUCK/Y, GOOD LUCK

Open hand shakes near chin
(can be both hands). If tongue
tip protrudes, means *careless.*
Can be thumb tip of 'L. hand
brushing nose.

MANNER/S, BEHAVIOUR

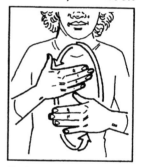

Flat hands brush alternately
backwards down body. With
head tilted and lips pressed
together, means *calm, patient,
tolerant.*

MAYBE, MIGHT, POSSIBLY

'Y' hand twists quickly from
wrist. Lips may be stretch. Can
be palm up flat hands moving
up and down alternately
(uncertain).

33

MEASURE, MEASUREMENT

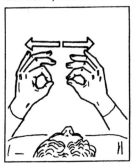

'O' hands move apart. May change direction/location in context. Also means *string*, *wire* (can be with small twisting movements.)

MEAT, BEEF, BUTCHER

Index prods into neck (can be twice), or bent index and thumb grasp cheek (also meaning *bare, flesh, insult*). As shown, also means *kill*.

MEDICINE, CHEMIST

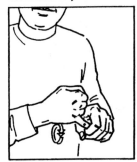

End of R. little finger makes forward circles inside opening of L. full 'O' hand. Also means *poison*.

MEET, FACE TO FACE

Extended indexes (person classifiers) move towards each other, located/directed to suit context. Without movement, meaning is *one to one*.

MESS, MESSY, UNTIDY

Open hands make alternating circles (tip of tongue between teeth), or palm up flat hands move alternately forward/down and apart.

MILK

Fists make repeated alternate up/down movements, may use slight squeezing action. Hands may rub against each other.

MIRROR, REFLECTION

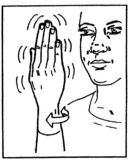

Flat hand makes very slight quick twisting movements in front of face. Eyegaze is towards hand.

MISS, ERROR, MISTAKE

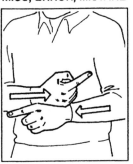

Indexes point and move in, R. brushing top of L., lips pressed together, or tips of 'V' hand prod neck (*miss, feel loss*). Regional.

MIX, MINGLE, BLEND

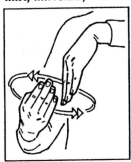

Bent hands circle alternately round each other. May vary in context.

MONEY, CASH, FINANCE

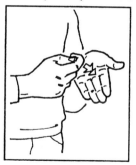

R. thumb tucked into bent index, taps L. palm twice. R. handshape may vary. Can be thumb of full 'C' hand on L. palm (*funds*).

MORNING, GOOD MORNING

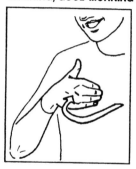

Tips of R. bent hand, thumb up, contact left then right upper chest. Can be bent hands, or closed hands moving up body (regional).

MOVE, SHIFT

Palm facing flat hands move firmly to the right. Will change in context. Movement in upward arc to the left gives *meanwhile*.

MOON

O' hand moves in crescent shape, as fingers open, then close. Also one version of *Pakistan*.

MOTHER, MUM, MUMMY

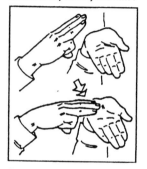

R. 'M' hand taps twice on L. palm. In some regions, 'M' hand taps side of forehead, or R. index taps back of L. ring finger twice.

MUST, COMPULSORY

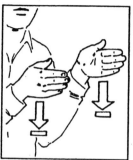

Palm facing flat hands move down emphatically, or closed hand moves sharply in, twisting to palm up. Also means *have to, should, ought*.

MORE

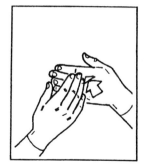

Palm back flat hands (L. hand can be closed). R. taps back of L. twice, or hands start in contact, then R. moves forward.

MOUNTAIN

Flat hands move up/in to contact each other at the tips. If the movement is reversed, the sign produced is *tent*.

MY OWN, MINE, MY

Closed hand taps chest twice (can be single contact), also means *belongs to me*. As shown also means *confess, repent, my fault*.

NAME, CALL, CALLED

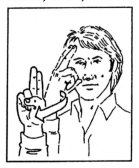

'N' hand on side of forehead, moves and twists forward, or palm facing 'V' hands move slightly outwards as fingers flex (*called, entitled*).

NAUGHTY, BOTHER

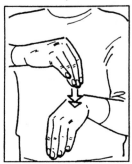

Tips of R. bent hand tap back of L. hand twice. Furrowed brow may be used.

NEAR, CLOSE, NOT FAR

R. index moves away from L. with small twist, or moves back towards L. Can be R. flat hand moving towards L., or other variation.

NEARLY, ALMOST

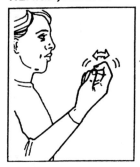

Thumb, and index tips touch; hand makes small movements back and forth, or thumb flicks off index (also *cheap, not much*). Eyes are narrowed

NEW, MODERN

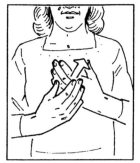

R. flat hand brushes up back (or front) of L. Can be repeated. also means *fashion* and *fresh* (R. hand fingers may open).

NEWSPAPER

Hands move up and apart, twisting to palm up. If tips of R. 'C' hand then move down L. palm, meaning is *article, column.*

NEXT, AFTER, THEN

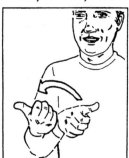

Closed hand, thumb extended twists over to palm up. Direction may change in context. Also means *neighbour, next door.*

NICE, SWEET, TASTY

Thumb tip moves across chin, (also *delicious, lovely*), or index of R. 'L' hand on cheek moves right and bends (also *lovely, pretty*).

NIGHT, EVENING, DARK

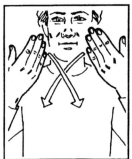

Palm back flat hands swing in/down to cross each other. One of many variations. Reversed movement gives *day, light.*

NO, DENY, REFUSE

Palm back closed hand twists sharply to palm forward, (accompanied by head shake). Can also mean *turn* (the head) *away*.

NOT, NO, DON'T

Flat hands start crossed then swing sharply apart, with head shake and furrowed brow. Also means *not allowed, finished, forbidden*.

NOW, PRESENT, TODAY

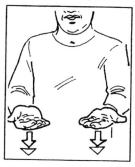

Palm up flat hands make short downward movement, twice. one sharp movement gives *at once, right now, immediately*.

NOISY, LOUD, SOUND

Index moves in forward circular movements at side of head. also means *London*.

NOT YET, BEFORE

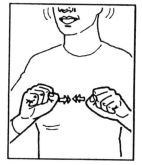

Closed hands, palm forward/down, shake in small quick side to side movements. Also means *wait* (or two small downward movements).

NUMBER, FIGURES, MATHS

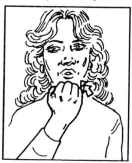

Knuckles of palm back closed hand tap chin twice (also *date*) or open hand held palm back with fingers wiggling.

NON-MANUAL FEATURES

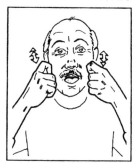

Thumbs tucked into bent indexes, hands move up/down alternately. Refers to grammatical use of *face/head/body/lip-patterns* in BSL.

NOTHING, NOBODY, NONE

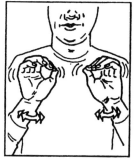

'O' hands, (or full 'O'), shake slightly, or make small inward circles, (head shakes and tongue tip may protrude). Can be one hand.

NURSE

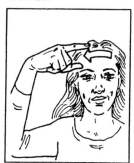

Palm back 'C' hand moves across forehead (regional). Can be index or thumb tip drawing cross on left upper arm, or other variations.

37

OFF, ABSENT

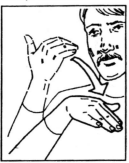

Palm back bent hand twists to point forward, palm down, at side of neck (regional).

OFF, GET OFF, ALIGHT

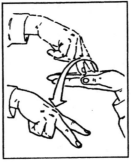

R. 'V' or bent 'V' hand (legs classifier), on L. palm, moves off in small arc (fingers may flex). Movement reversed for *get on, board.*

OLD, AGED, ELDERLY

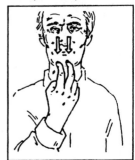

Palm back 'V' hand (or bent 'V'), moves down in front of nose as fingers flex, or hand bends backwards. Also means *dark, night* (regional).

ON, PLACE ON, PUT ON

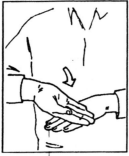

Back of R. flat hand moves down onto back of L. flat hand. Will vary in context.

ONLY, ONLY ONE, ALONE

L. hand palm back, R. index extended moves down/right behind L. palm.

OPEN , OPENING, LAUNCH

Palm back flat hands touch at tips, then swing to point forward. Will vary in context.

OPERATION, SURGERY

Tip of extended thumb moves across appropriate part of body, e.g. *hip operation* on the hip, *heart surgery* on the chest, etc.

ORANGE

Palm forward (or palm left), clawed hand opens and closes at side of mouth, or fingers may flex. Refers to the colour, fruit or drink.

OUR, OURS, OUR OWN

Closed hand sweeps round in arc from left to right side of chest (can be both hands moving apart/back to chest). Also means *belong to us.*

OUTSIDE, OUTDOOR/S

Bent hand moves forward twice. Also means *abroad, foreign* (right arm may rest on L. hand). A firm movement gives *pester* (directional).

OVER, OVERTIME

R. bent hand moves over L. in small arc. Refers to over in the sense of value, quantity, number, age etc.

PAINT, PAINTER

R. 'N' hand brushes up and down L. palm. Can be R. hand only. R. flat hand can be used or other in context.

PAPER, PIECE OF PAPER

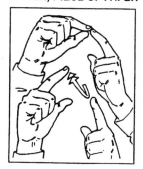

R. index and thumb tip flick against tip of L. index, twice, or brush forward twice off tip of L. index, or several other variations.

PARK, GARDEN, GREEN

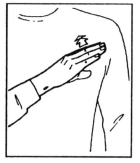

Index edge of R. flat hand taps left upper chest twice. Also means *Burwood Park School*, and is a regional sign for *school*.

PARTY, ENTERTAINMENT

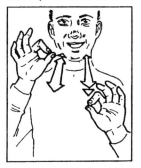

'O' hands move alternately up and down to mouth, or move in and out near waist (also *dance*). Or 'Y' hands twist in circles near head.

PEAR

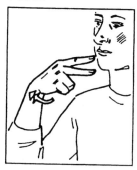

'V' hand brushes forwards twice at side of chin, or palm left R. 'N' hand twists to palm back at side of mouth, or other variation.

PEAS, SHELLING PEAS

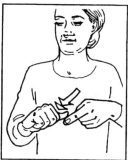

R. thumb scrapes forward twice along extended L. index finger. Regional. One of several variations.

PEN, BIRO, OFFICE

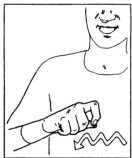

Tip of R. index and thumb in contact, as hand moves in writing action ('O' hand may be used). Also means *pencil, signature, write.*

39

PENCIL, PEN, WRITE

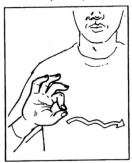

'O' hand moves in writing action. May start from above ear, or fingers of palm back 'N' hand flick up/down in front of nose (regional *pencil*).

PENNY, PENCE

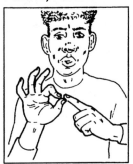

Hands form fingerspelt letter 'P'.

PEOPLE, HUMAN, PUBLIC

Index and thumb stroke chin, then index brushes forward on cheek, or palm forward index moves down in sharp zig-zag, or other variations.

PERHAPS, POSSIBLY

'Y' hand twists quickly at wrist, or palm up flat hands move up/down alternately, with stretched lips and tilted head (also *might, maybe*).

PET, CAT, STROKE

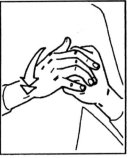

R. hand strokes down back of L. closed hand twice. Regional.

PHOTO, COPY

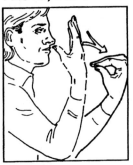

Palm back hand in front of face, moves forward as fingers close onto thumb. Directional.

PICK, CHOOSE, SELECT

Index closes onto thumb in short backward movement, (can be both hands alternately). Directional.

PICNIC, BUFFET, FEAST

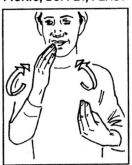

Bunched hands make alternate repeated movements to the mouth.

PICTURE, CHART, POSTER

Index fingers move apart, down, then together in outline of shape.

PILL, TABLET

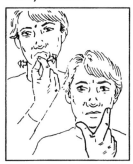

R. index and thumb flick open, twice, near mouth. R. hand may start in contact with L. palm, before moving to mouth.

PIG, PORK

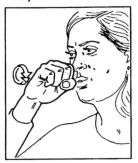

Fist makes small circles near nose, or palm back clawed hand moves forward from nose, (wrinkled nose gives *greedy, selfish*).

PINK

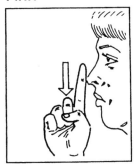

Index extended from full 'O' hand, (little finger may also be extended) brushes down nose, or brushes left across nose, twice.

PLAY, GAME

Open hands make simultaneous circular movements, upwards/apart, or brush palm to palm, up and down against each other.

PLEASE, IF YOU PLEASE

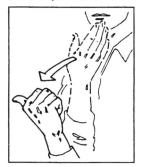

Tips of flat hand touch mouth; hand moves forward/down as fingers close down to palm. Can be made without final closing movement.

PLEASED, APPRECIATE

Flat hand rubs in circles on chest, or palm facing hands brush together, twice, (also *enjoy, glad, happy*). Face/body show positive expression.

POLICE, POLICE OFFICER

Fingers of R. 'V' hand flex as tips are drawn across back of L. wrist.

POLITE, MANNER/S

Index moves from mouth, to flat hand brushing down body, or both hands brush alternately down body, or other variation.

POOR, POVERTY, SCRUFFY

Tips of R. clawed hand scratch along forearm, twice. R. index moves sharply left, down left forearm for *bankrupt, poor, poverty*.

41

POORLY, UNWELL

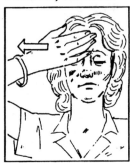

Flat hand brushes across forehead, or R. index contacts forehead, then taps twice on L. index, pointing right, or other variations.

POTATO, PEEL, SPUD

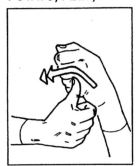

R. thumb scrapes L. fist, twice, or tips of bent R. 'V' tap back of L. (also *Ireland*), or R. fingers/thumb close together, off L. fist.

PULL, TUG

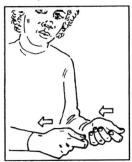

Thumbs tucked into bent indexes, hands move back/right simultaneaously. Body may move back. Will vary in context.

PURPLE

R. 'O' hand brushes tip of L. index, twice, or R. flat hand touches lips then rubs in circles on L. palm or back of hand, or other (all regional).

PUSH, SHOVE

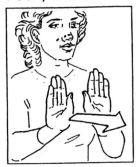

Flat hands and body push forward (will change to suit context). If body moves back, head to one side, the meaning is *rebuff, resist*.

PUT, TO PLACE

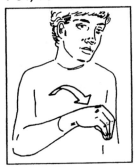

Bunched hand moves in sideways arc. Handshape and movement will change according to referents in context.

QUICK, BE QUICK, EARLY

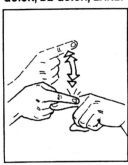

R. index bounces sharply up off L. index, or can be quick, repeated contact (*fast, hurry up*). Also means *emergency, sudden, urgent*.

QUIET, BE QUIET, PEACE

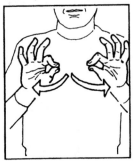

Tips of 'O'; hands touch, then move down/apart (may start crossed). May start with index on pressed together lips, or with 'Sh' lip-pattern.

RABBIT

Palm forward 'N' hands, held at either side of head, bend from palm knuckles, several times.

42

RADIO, WIRELESS

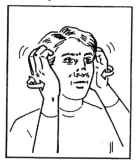

Clawed hands, over ears, make quick twisting movements from wrists. Can be one hand. Hands may tap against head *(audiology)*.

RAIN, RAINING, DOWNPOUR

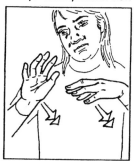

Open hands move simultaneously down several times. Puffed cheeks and firm movement down/left give *heavy rain, downpour*.

READ, SCAN

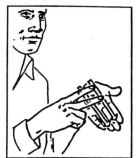

R. 'V' hand moves across L. palm, or in manner to suit context (fingers represent eye gaze), or sign **book** moves side to side near face.

READY, PREPARED

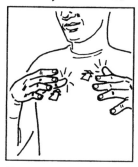

Thumbs of palm down open hands (or one hand), tap upper chest twice, (can be upward brushing movements). Also means *already*.

REAL/LY, SURE, TRUE

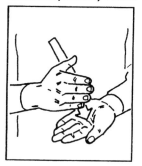

Blade of R. flat hand hits L. palm repeated for *actually, really, surely, truly*, or tip of R. extended thumb twists into L. palm *(real/ly*, regional).

RED

Index brushes twice down lip, bending slightly. Can be single firm movement, or index pointing left moves left across chin (regional).

REMEMBER, MEMORY

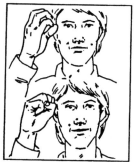

Clawed hand closes sharply to a fist at side of head, or index on forehead, than bent (or closed) hands tap together twice, R. on top of L.

RIGHT, CORRECT, PROPER

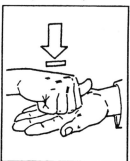

R. closed hand, thumb out, hits L. palm. May contact chest *(I'm right)*, or move and face forward *(you're right)*, and so on.

RIVER, BROOK, STREAM

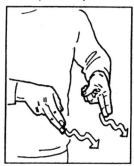

'N' hands held palm facing, pointing forward/down, move forward with small side to side movements. Flat hands can be used.

43

ROAD, AVENUE, STREET

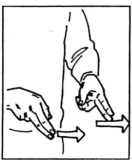

Palm facing 'N' hands (or flat hands), pointing down, twist to point and move forward. Also means *method, path, style, system, way*.

ROOM, STUDIO

Indexes point down, (or sometimes point up), and move apart, and then back, in outline shape, or flat hands move in outline shape.

RUBBISH, RIDICULOUS

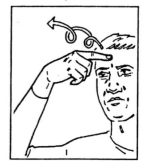

R. index on forehead, twists sharply up/right in spirals, or bent hand moves up sharply to left armpit, or other variation. Nose is wrinkled.

RUBBISH, TRASH, WASTE

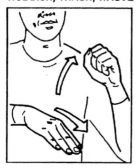

L. hand moves upwards, closing to a fist, as R. full 'O' hand moves down, springing open. Can be R. only. One of several variations.

RUDE, BAD MANNERED

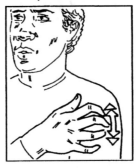

Tips of R. clawed hand rub up and down, twice on left upper arm (or on left or right side of upper chest). Also means *impolite, impudent*.

RUDE, CRUDE, OFFENSIVE

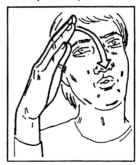

Palm left R. flat hand twists sharply to palm down in front of nose (school sign), or thumb and bent index grasp cheek, or other variation.

RUN, RUNNER, ATHLETE

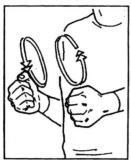

Closed hands make alternate forward circular or up/down movements, or palm back closed hands with indexes flexing move forward.

SAD, DEPRESS, FEEL DOWN

Index edge of R. flat hand moves down chest, or front of nose, palm left (*serious, solemn*) or other variation. Mouth and shoulders droop.

SALAD

Hands closed with index, middle fingers and thumbs extended, make inward circular tossing movements (open hands may be used).

44

SAME, SIMILAR, TOO

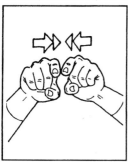

Indexes extended and pointing forward, tap together twice (can be single contact), or R. 'N' hand touches nose, then L. palm (regional)

SAND, ASHES, SOIL

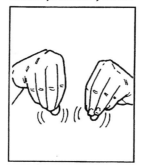

Thumbs rub across pads of fingers several times (also *earth, flour, powder*). Formation may also move upwards.

SANDWICH, BUTTY

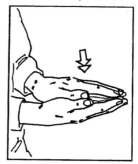

Flat hands held palms together, R. hand taps L. twice, or palm back bunched hands held together near mouth move slightly side to side.

SAY, COMMENT, TELL

Index moves forward from mouth, or full 'O' hands spring open twice, either palm forward, or palm back (directional).

SCHOOL

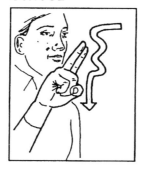

Palm forward 'N' hand moves down in side to side movement, or palm back flat hand shakes side to side near mouth, or other variation.

SEA, OCEAN, WATER

Palm down open hand moves to the right with short up and down movements. Both hands can be used, moving apart.

SECOND/LY, ANOTHER

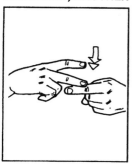

Middle finger of R. 'V' hand taps L. index twice, or palm forward 'V' hand twists to palm back, or a number of other regional variations.

SEE, LOOK, SIGHT

Index moves forward from eye (can be 'V' hand). If palm back and tapping under eye with mouth slightly open, means *let's see, check out.*

SELF, MYSELF

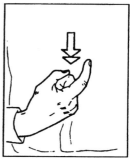

R. index extended, palm up/right, brushes twice down body. Also means *alone, individual, personal, personally.*

45

SHAME, PITY, SYMPATHY

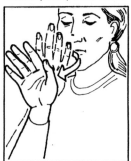

Palm down flat hand makes small forward circular stroking movements. Also means *paternal, patronising* (tongue between teeth).

SHARE, DIVIDE

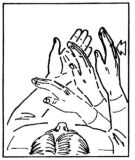

Blade of R. flat hand taps along L. palm several times, or rests on L. palm as formation moves back and forth, twice. May vary in context.

SHARP, FAST, SPEED

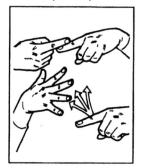

R. index contacts L. index, then moves sharply away as fingers spring open.

SHEEP

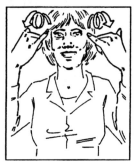

Extended little fingers held at sides of head, move forward/down in circular movement. One hand may be used. Also means *Derby*.

SHIRT, COLLAR, SOLICITOR

Hands move down as indexes close onto thumbs, or other variation. Palm back 'V' hands move down/apart under neck for *lawyer, solicitor*.

SHOE

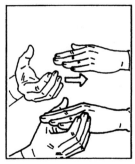

Palm up R. full 'C' hand moves left to slot onto fingers of L. hand. May vary.

SHOP, SHOPPING

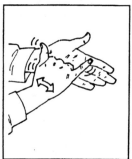

R. 'Y' hand rubs side to side on L. palm (also means *New York*). or palm down bent hands makes small downward movement. Regional.

SHORTS

Blades of palm up flat hands tap twice against upper thighs.

SHOULD, MUST, OUGHT

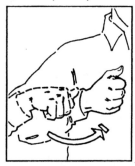

Palm down closed hand moves down/in, with stress, twisting to palm back (also *compulsory, mandatory*), with lips pressed, means *blast*.

SHOW, DEMONSTRATE

Palm back flat hands below eyes, move forward, down and apart. Also means *display, exhibit/ion, expose, open, prove.*

SICK, VOMIT

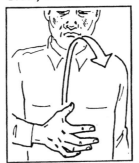

R. open hand brushes up body and forward from mouth, or other variations. Clawed hand rubs stomach in circles for feel *sick, queasy.*

SIGN, SIGN LANGUAGE

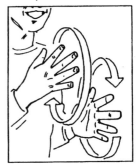

Open hands move in alternate forward circles (can rub together), or twist forwards and back sharply *(chat)*, or other changes in context.

SILLY, COMIC, DAFT

Extended middle finger makes two short, firm movements towards side of forehead. Nose is wrinkled.

SING, SINGER

'N' hands move forward/up from mouth in circular movements. 'V' hands may be used, or index edge of fist held to mouth *(microphone).*

SISTER

Edge of bent index taps nose twice. Bent index on nose flicks straight, or hand makes small downward twist for two regional variations.

SIT, SEAT, SIT DOWN

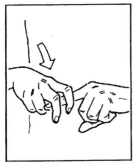

Fingers of R. bent 'V' (or 'N' hand) hook over L. index, or palm down fists move down, or palm down flat hands, R. on L. move down.

SKIRT

Flat hands move down/apart from sides of waist, or blades of palm up flat hands move apart across upper thighs *(mini skirt).* May vary.

SKY, HEAVEN

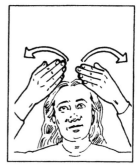

Flat hands move down/back, move apart in small arc above head.

47

SLEEP, ASLEEP

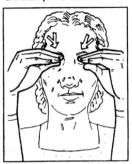

Fingers of bent hands (or 'N' hands, or indexes). close onto thumbs near eyes, or palm in clawed hand snaps shut across eyes, (fast asleep, oversleep).

SLOW/LY, AGES, LONG

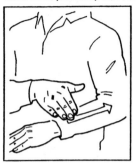

R, flat hand (or index finger) moves slowly up left forearm, or palm down open hand waves downwards twice (slowly, slow down).

SOCIAL WORKER, WELFARE

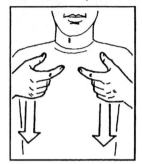

Tips of palm back 'C' hands move down upper chest (also missioner). May repeat. Can be fingerspelt 'SW'.

SOCK/S

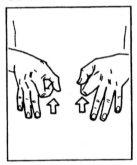

Palm back 'O' hands make short upward movement in front of body. May repeat. May twist from palm down to palm back.

SOME, FEW, SEVERAL

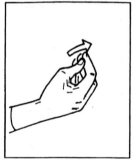

Pad of thumb rubs across tips of fingers from little finger to index, or index and thumb tip rub together several times.

SOON, NOT LONG

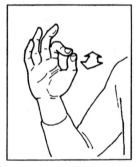

'O' hand moves slightly back and forth twice (also one version of special). Can be palm up with other fingers closed, (nearly, almost).

SORRY, APOLOGY, REGRET

Closed hand rubs in small circles on chest (can be edge of extended little finger), or palm in clawed hand shakes back and forth near head.

SOUP, SOUP SPOON

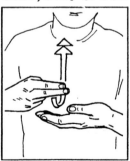

R. 'N' hand (or thumb tucked into bent index) moves upwards to mouth, twice, twisting to palm up. Also means cereal, porridge.

SPEECH, SPEAK, SPOKEN

Fingers of 'N' (or 'V') hand open and close onto thumb in short forward movements, or index makes small forward circles near mouth.

48

SPOIL, DAMAGE, IMPAIR

R. little finger moves sharply down against L. as both twist to point down, or open hands, R. on L. twist against each other to reverse places.

SPOON

Thumb tucked into bent index; hand moves to mouth (also *pudding, sweet, porridge, cereal*). May vary in context.

SPRING (season)

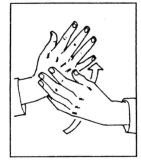

R. open hand swivels to point up from behind L. hand, or R. full 'O' hand opens as it moves up behind L. (also *bloom, create, develop*).

STAND, WAIT

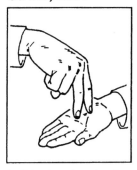

R. 'V' hand stands on L. palm. Formation moves down firmly for *stand firm, take a stand*, or with small repeated movements *(wait ages)*.

START, BEGIN, COMMENCE

R. extended thumb brushes sharply down behind L. hand, or palm down open hands snap shut, twisting sharply to palm forward.

STAY, REMAIN, BE STILL

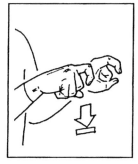

Palm down 'C' hands make small firm movement down (can be one hand). or bent indexes linked together move firmly down (also *stick, stuck*).

STOP, HALT, WAIT

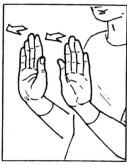

Palm forward flat hands make short firm movement forward (can be one hand), may be repeated, also meaning *wait, hang on, hold on*.

STRONG, ENERGY, POWER

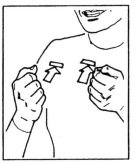

Fists make short firm movement backwards, bending from elbows, or R. index moves in forward arc down left upper arm *(muscle)*.

SUMMER, STRANGER

Index edge of bent hand touches chin, then forehead, or is drawn across forehead to the right (*heat, summer*), or other variation.

SUN/NY, SUNSHINE, LIGHT

Palm in full 'O' hand makes short movement in/down, as it springs open at head height, or located to suit context. Also means *beam, ray.*

SUNDAY, PRAY, PRAYER

Flat hands tap together twice *(Sunday)*, or are held together *(pray, prayer, chapel, church),* or other regional variation.

SWEET/S, TOFFEE

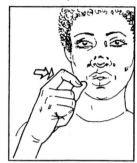

Tips of index and thumb in contact, tap side of mouth twice, or tip of extended index twists repeatedly against side of mouth. Regional.

SWIM, SWIMMING

Flat hands move forward/apart in repeated circular movements, or arms move in overarm strokes. As shown also means *breast-stroke.*

TABLE, ALTAR, BOARD

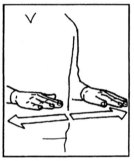

Palm down flat hands move apart. Also means *flat, ground, level, platform, slab.*

TAKE, ADOPT/ION, GET

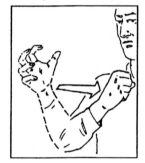

Palm left R. clawed hand moves left as it snaps shut, (also *achieve/ment),* or starts palm down closing in backward movement. Directional.

TALK, CHAT, DISCUSS

Closed hands, indexes extended; R. taps L. twice after touching mouth, or fingers of bent hand open and close onto thumbs twice. Varies.

TAXI, CAB

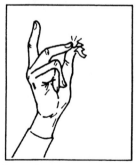

Middle finger and thumb tip click together twice, hand held at head height. One of several variations.

TEA, CUPPA

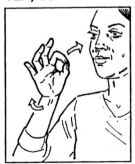

Palm left R. 'O' hand tips backwards near mouth, or same movement with closed hand, thumb tucked into bent index. Also means *cafe, cup.*

50

TEACH/ER, INSTRUCT/OR

Indexes contact sides of mouth, then make two short movements forward, down an apart. May vary.

THAN

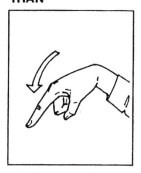

Index finger makes sharp downward movement, diagonally down/in. Regional.

THAT'S ALL, ONLY

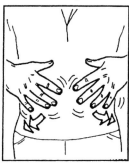

Palm back open hands shake downwards quickly twice, or palm forward open hands are held near shoulders. Shoulders are slightly raised.

TELEPHONE, CALL, RING

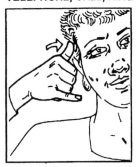

'Y' hand moves to ear. May move down onto body (*call me*) or forward (*I'll 'phone*), or sign for *minicom, textphone* moves forward or back.

THANK YOU, APPRECIATE

Tips of flat hand contact mouth, then move forward/ down, or both hands move forward/down and apart. Also means *grateful, thank, thankful.*

THIEF, THIEVE, PINCH

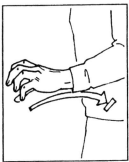

Palm down clawed hand snatches sharply backwards to palm back at side of body. Also means *nick, steal, and rob, robber/y* (both hands).

TELEVISION, TELLY, TV

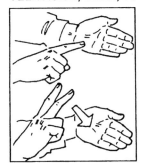

Fingerspell 'TV', or indexes held together and pointing forward, move apart and down in outlines shape (also *monitor, screen*).

THAT, THERE, THIS

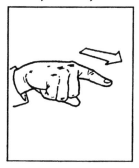

Index makes short movement forward/down, accompanied by eyegaze. Short repeated movement gives *that one, this one.*

THING, ENTITY, ISSUE

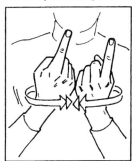

Closed hands with indexes extended, twist slightly round and tap together twice. May tap repeatedly, moving to the right (*issues*). 51

THINK, JUDGE, OPINION

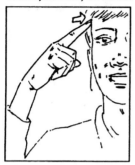

Index taps forehead. May make small circles (also *imagine, mull over, ponder, presume*) brows furrowed, or tap twice (*sensible*), brows raised.

THIRSTY, FANCY, WISH

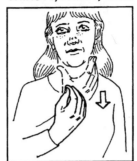

Fingers and thumb on throat, move down closing to bunched hand (with open mouth, also *crave, desire, lust*), or index moves down throat.

THIS, HERE

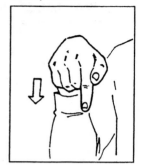

Index pointing down, makes small downward movement (may repeat), both hands can be used. Also means *down, downstairs, south*.

THROUGH, ACCESS

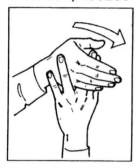

R. flat hand moves forward/left between middle and ring fingers (or index and middle fingers) of L. hand. Also one version of *between*.

TIDY

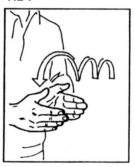

Palm facing flat hands move right in small hops (single hop left gives *meanwhile*), or 'N' hand taps side of nose twice (*posh, smart*). Will vary.

TIME, WHAT TIME?

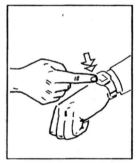

R. index taps back of L. wrist twice, or fingers of open hand wiggle, or R. index on L.palm wiggles (also *clock*). Eyebrows raised if question.

TIRED, EXHAUSTED, WEARY

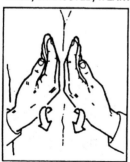

Palm back bent hands on chest, flop down to palm up (can be open hands), or little fingers move down chest. Cheeks may be puffed.

TOAST, GRILL

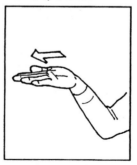

Palm up flat hand moves forward, or tips of R. 'V' hand tap L. palm twice (also *fork*). Will vary.

TODAY, NOW, NOWADAYS

Palm up flat hands make two short movements towards each other (or downwards), or tips of R. bent hand tap L. palm (regional *now, still*).

TOILET

R. index of fingerspelt 'T' taps L; blade (or palm) twice (also *teetotal, Tuesday*), or thumb of 'Y' hand brushes chest twice. Many variations.

TOMATO

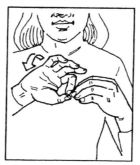

Tips of R. 'O' hand twist forward against tips of L. bunched hand. One of several variations.

TOMORROW, NEXT DAY

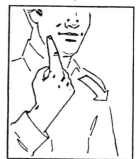

Index tip touches side of chin, then swings forward/down to finish palm up. With middle finger also extended, means in *two days time*.

TOP, IMPORTANT, V.I.P.

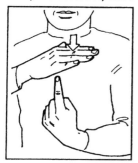

Palm of R. flat hand moves down onto tip of L. index, hands may be held at head height. Contact may be repeated (also *crucial, vital*).

TOWN, PLACE

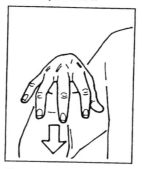

Clawed hand moves down slightly (palm forward with slight twist gives one version of *country, region*), or 'O' hand makes small circles.

TRAFFIC, TAILBACK

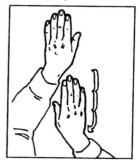

Palm down flat hands (vehicle classifiers), R. moves back in short hops, or both jerk slowly forward (*gridlock, jam*). Will vary in context.

TRAIN, RAILWAY STATION

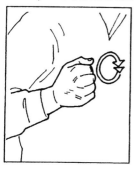

Palm left R. closed hand makes small forward circles, or short, firm movement forward. May vary in context.

TREE

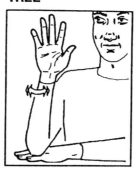

Right forearm held upright, resting on L. hand, R. open hand twists repeatedly from wrist. Formation moves round in arc for *forest, wood*.

TROUBLE, BOTHER, NAUGHTY

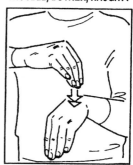

Tips of R. bent hand tap back of L. twice (one tap, twisting to palm up gives *not bothered*), or flat hands slap forearms alternately (regional).

53

TROUSERS

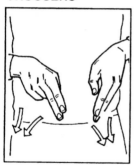

'N' hands move down together in front of right side of waist, then left side of waist, or closed hands move upwards at sides of hips.

TRY, ATTEMPT, EFFORT

R. index brushes forward against L. Can be repeated. Single sharp movement gives *majority, most, mostly* and *special, very* (regional).

UNDER, OVEN, ROAST

L. flat hand, fingers pointing to the right. R. flat hand, fingers pointing away from signer moves under L. in small arc. R. hand only means *grill*.

UNTIL, FINALLY

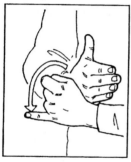

R. flat hand moves forward/over L. hand to land on extended little finger. Also one version of *weekend*.

UP, UPSTAIRS, NORTH

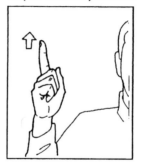

R. index finger makes small movement up. If repeated, movement means *upstairs*.

USE, USEFUL

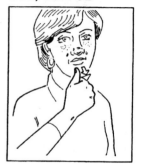

Thumb brushes twice down chin, (or can be tips of bent hand).

VERY

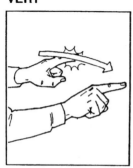

Two indexes pointing forward. R. index brushes forward contacting L. index in one sharp movement.

VOICE, THROAT

Tips of 'N' hand tap voice box twice.

WAIT, HANG ON

Palm down bent hands make short firm downward movement. If movement is repeated means regional sign for *shop, shopping, London*.

54

WALK

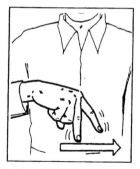

Index and middle fingers move like legs walking. One of several variations. If fingers move up/away means *stairs, go upstairs*; down/away means *go downstairs*.

WANT, NEED, WISH

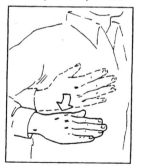

Flat hand on side of upper chest brushes down, twisting to palm down in small movement. Also means *desire, hope*.

DON'T WANT

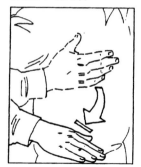

Flat hand on side of upper chest brushes sharply down and away from body, with emphasis accompanied with headshake.

WASH HANDS

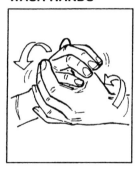

Two full 'C' hands mime appropriate washing action. Means wash face. If flat hand, palm facing signer, makes small anti-clockwise circle, around face.

WATCH ME, PAY ATTENTION

Two 'V' hands pointing forward, twist back toward signer with stress.

WE, US

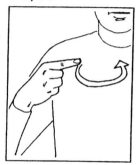

Index held on side of chest makes movement in a forward arc to land on opposite side of chest.

WEAR, BODY

Open hands start on chest then brush down body. Can be one hand only.

LAST WEEK, ONE WEEK AGO

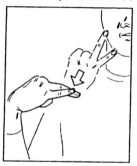

'7' formation hand; ring fingertip touches side of chin then moves down ending with fingertips touching right shoulder. Regional.

NEXT WEEK

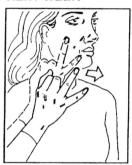

'7' formation hand; ring fingertip touches side of chin then makes small movement away from signer.

55

THIS WEEK

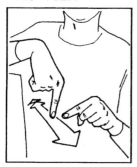

Index fingers, pointing down, makes movement forward and back twice.

WEEKEND

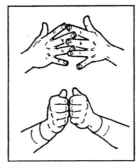

Hands from brief fingerspelt 'W', pull slightly apart, and close together *(agree)* or blade of R. hand moves down left arm onto L. little finger. Regional.

WET, DAMP, MOIST

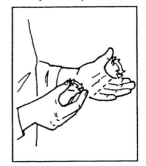

Palm up bent hands open and close onto ball of thumbs twice. One hand may be used.

WHAT?, WHAT FOR?

Index extended; Palm forward, moves side to side in short quick movements. Face and body indicate question form. Also a Regional sign for *Why?*

WHEN?, WHAT TIME?

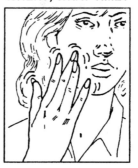

Open hand on side of cheek; fingers wiggle repeatedly. Face and body indicate question form.

WHERE?, WHEREABOUTS?

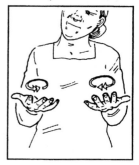

Open hands, palms up make inward circular movements, or in/out towards each other. Face/body indicate question form.

WHITE

Tips of 'O' hand make short repeated downward brushing movement near to the neck. The index fingertip can be used.

WHO?

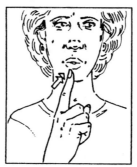

Palm left R. index (can be bent index) contacts chin twice, or thumb of 'L' hand on chin, index flexes. Regional. Lips are rounded, face/body indicate question form.

WHY, BECAUSE

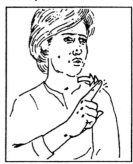

Edge of extended R. index taps left shoulder twice. Face and body indicate if question form.

WILL, WOULD, SHALL

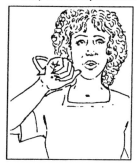

Palm forward closed hand twists to palm down, while maintaining contact on side of cheek. Can be same movement with tip of extended index on cheek.

WIN, SUCCEED, ACHIEVE

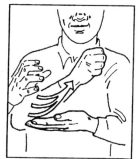

Palm left R. clawed hand moves sharply across L. palm and closes to a fist. Can be R. hand only at head height or other variation.

WINDOW

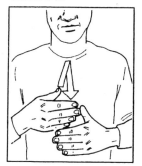

Palm back flat hands, R. on top of L., R. hand moves up then down back onto L. hand.

WINTER, COLD

Closed hands make repeated short movement towards each other. The shoulders are hunched.

WITH, TOGETHER

Index, middle finger and thumb of L. hand move over fingers of R. 'N' hand and close.

WOMAN, FEMALE

Edge of index brushes forward, twice, on cheek. Also means *girlfriend, lady* and a regional sign for *always*.

WON'T, WOULDN'T, REFUSE

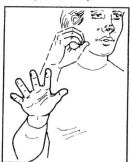

Fingers flexed behind thumb; hand moves sharply forward from side of chin as fingers spring to open hand. Accompanied by headshake.

WORD

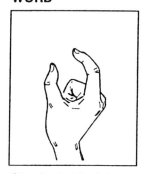

'C' hand, palm left, pointing away from signer. No movement.

WORK, JOB, CAREER

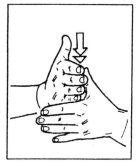

Blade of R. flat hand chops repeatedly down on index edge of L. flat hand, at right angles. Small sawing action gives regional sign for *wood*. 57

WORSE

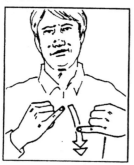

R. little fingertip brushes forward /down against L. little fingertip, twice. Can also be both little fingers start crossed then make short movement down and apart together.

WRITE/R, AUTHOR

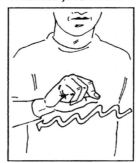

Index and thumb held together move up and down while moving to the right. Can also be L. flat hand held under R. hand. Also means *notes, secretary*.

WRONG, EVIL, SIN

Side of R. little finger taps L. palm twice (raised eyebrows for *what's wrong?*). May start with tips of open hand on chin. Can be R. hand only directed forward *(You're wrong)* or on chest *(I'm wrong)*.

YELLOW

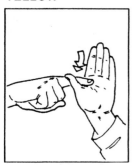

Hands in fingerspelt 'Y' formation; index finger makes repeated downward brushing movement on L. thumb. Can be palm in clawed hand held at side of head makes several, short, quick twisting movements (Regional).

YES

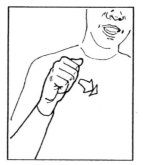

Closed hand makes repeated movement down, may rest across L. index. Can be palm back (directional). Head nods.

YESTERDAY

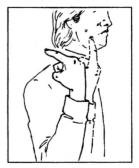

Palm back bent index on side of chin moves down/back, or moves to point back over shoulder. Middle finger also extended gives two days ago etc.

YOGHURT

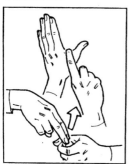

Fingerspelt 'Y' formation followed by 'N' hand moving up from full 'O' hand, as if miming eating from pot.

YOU

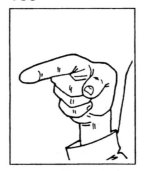

Extended index finger makes short movement forward or towards person concerned. For plural, hand sweeps round in small horizontal arc.

ZEBRA-CROSSING

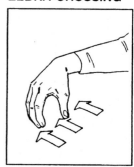

Palm down full 'C' hand makes repeated short movements to the right, while moving away from the signer after each short movement. Can be two hands.

VOCABULARY INDEX
(FIRST WORD)

1 ABOUT (approx.)
   ABOUT (concerning)
   ACCIDENT
   ADD
   ADDRESS (live)
   AEROPLANE
   AFTER
   AFTERNOON
   AGAIN

2 ALL
   ALWAYS
   AMBULANCE
   AND
   ANGRY
   ANIMAL
   ANOTHER
   ANSWER
   ANY

3 APPLE
   ARGUE
   ASK
   AUTUMN
   AWAY
   BABY
   BACKWARDS
   BAD (terrible)
   BAG

4 BAKED BEANS
   BALL
   BALLOON
   BANANA
   BANDAGE
   BAT/TING
   BATH/ING
   BEAR
   BEAUTIFUL

5 BECAUSE
   BED
   BEEFBURGER
   BEFORE (prior)
   BEFORE (past)
   BEHAVE
   BELL
   BELT
   BEST

6 BETTER
   BETWEEN
   BICYCLE
   BIG
   BIRD
   BIRTHDAY
   BISCUIT
   BLACK (person)
   BLANKET

7 BLIND
   BLOOD
   BLOUSE
   BLUE
   BOAT
   BODY
   BOIL
   BOOK (catalogue)
   BOTTLE

8 BOWL (sink)
   BOX
   BOY
   BREAD
   BREAK (snap)
   BREAKFAST
   BRIGHT (clear)
   BRING
   BROTHER

9 BROWN
   BRUSH (hairbrush)
   BUILD/ING
   BUS
   BUSY
   BUT
   BUTTER
   BUTTERFLY
   BUY

10 CABBAGE
   CAKE
   CAN (able)
   CAN'T
   CAR
   CAREFUL/LY
   CARPET
   CARROT
   CARRY

11 CAT
   CAULIFLOWER
   CHAIR
   CHANGE (alter)
   CHANGE (cash)
   CHEESE
   CHEW
   CHICKEN
   CHILDREN

12 CHIPS
   CHOCOLATE
   CHOOSE
   CHRISTMAS (Santa)
   CHURCH
   CINEMA
   CLASS/ROOM
   CLEAN
   CLEVER

13 CLIMB/ER
   CLOCK
   CLOSE (door)
   CLOTHES
   COAT
   COFFEE
   COLD (chilly)
   COLD (flu)
   COLOUR

14 COME
   CONTINUE
   COOK
   COOKER
   COOKERY
   COOL (air)
   CORNFLAKES
   COUGH
   COUNT

15 COUNTRYSIDE
   COW
   CRASH
   CRY
   CUCUMBER
   CULTURE
   CUPBOARD
   CUSTARD
   CUT BACK/OFF

16 CUTLERY	21 FIRE	26 HANDICAP (disability)
DANCE	FIRST	HAPPEN
DAY	FISH (a)	HAPPY (enjoy)
DEAD	FISH FINGERS	HARD / TO DO
DEAF / PERSON	FIX (firm)	HAVE
DIFFERENT	FIX (mend)	HE
DINNER	FLOWER	HEAR
DIRT/Y	FOG	HEARING / PERSON
DO	FOLLOW (go along with)	HEARING AID
17 DOCTOR	22 FOOD	27 HELLO
DOG	FOOTBALL/ER	HELP
DOLE	FOREVER	HER/S
DON'T	FORGET/FUL	HERE
DOOR	FORK	HIDE
DOWN	FRIEND	HOLD / ONTO
DRAW (sketch)	FRIGHTENED	HOLIDAY
DRAWER/S	FROM	HOME
DREAM	FRONT	HORSE
18 DRESS	23 FRUIT	28 HOSPITAL
DRINK	FULL	HOT
DROP	FUNNY (laugh)	HOUR/LY
DRY	FURNITURE	HOUSE
EASTER	GAME	HOW OLD?
EASY	GARDEN/ER	HUNGRY
EAT	GAS (fuel)	HURRY UP
EGG	GET	HURT
ELECTRIC/ITY	GIRL	I
19 EMPTY	24 GIVE	29 ICE CREAM
END	GLASSES (specs)	IF
ENOUGH	GLOVE/S	IN/TO
EVERYTHING	GLUE	INSIDE
FALL / OVER	GO / AWAY	JUG
FAMILY	GOING TO	JUMPER
FARM/ER	GOOD	JUST / NOW
FAST	GOOD MORNING	KEEP
FAT	GOODBYE	KEY
20 FATHER	25 GRANDFATHER	30 KICK / OUT
FAVOURITE	GRANDMOTHER	KISS
FED UP	GRASS	KITCHEN
FEEL (emotion)	GREED/Y	KNIFE
FIELD (meadow)	GREEN	KNOW/LEDGE
FIGHT	GREY	DON'T KNOW
FIND	GROW / UP	LATE
FINGERSPELL	GUESS	LAZY
FINISH	HALF	LEAD/ER

31	LEARN	36	NAME	41	PILL (tablet)
	LEAVE		NAUGHTY		PIG
	LEMONADE		NEAR		PINK
	LET (give permission)		NEARLY		PLAY (game)
	LETTER (mail)		NEW		PLEASE
	LIE / DOWN		NEWSPAPER		PLEASED
	LIE (untruth)		NEXT		POLICE / OFFICER
	LIGHT (day,dawn)		NICE		POLITE
	LIGHT (lamp)		NIGHT		POOR (poverty)

32	LIKE (approve)	37	NO (refuse)	42	POORLY
	DON'T LIKE		NOISY		POTATO
	LISTEN		NON-MANUAL		PULL
	LITTLE (bit)		FEATURES		PURPLE
	LONG / TIME		NOT		PUSH
	LONG TIME AGO		NOT YET		PUT
	LOOK		NOTHING		QUICK
	LOTTERY (nat. lottery)		NOW		QUIET
	LOUD		NUMBER		RABBIT
			NURSE		

33	LOVE			43	RADIO
	LOVELY	38	OFF (absent)		RAIN/ING
	LUCK/Y		OFF (get off)		READ
	MAKE (create)		OLD		READY
	MAN		ON		REAL/LY
	MANNER/S		ONLY/ONE		RED
	MANY		OPEN/ING		REMEMBER
	MATTER (what's the)		OPERATION		RIGHT (correct)
	MAYBE		ORANGE		RIVER
			OUR/S		

34	MEASURE/MENT			44	ROAD
	MEAT	39	OUTSIDE		ROOM
	MEDICINE		OVER/TIME		RUBBISH (ridiculous)
	MEET		PAINT/ER		RUBBISH (waste)
	MESS/Y		PAPER (piece of)		RUDE (bad mannered)
	MILK		PARK (garden)		RUDE (crude)
	MIRROR		PARTY		RUN/NER
	MISS (error)		PEAR		SAD
	MIX		PEAS		SALAD
			PEN		

35	MONEY			45	SAME
	MOON	40	PENCIL		SAND
	MORE		PENNY (pence)		SANDWICH
	MORNING		PEOPLE		SAY
	MOTHER		PERHAPS		SCHOOL
	MOUNTAIN		PET		SEA (ocean)
	MOVE		PHOTO		SECOND/LY
	MUST		PICK		SEE
	MY OWN		PICNIC		SELF
			PICTURE		

46 SHAME (pity)	51 TEACH/ER	56 THIS WEEK
SHARE	TELEPHONE	WEEKEND
SHARP	TELEVISION	WET
SHEEP	THAN	WHAT / FOR?
SHIRT	THANK YOU	WHEN?
SHOE	THAT	WHERE/ABOUTS?
SHOP/PING	THAT'S ALL	WHITE
SHORTS	THIEF	WHO?
SHOULD	THING	WHY?
47 SHOW (demonstrate)	52 THINK	57 WILL (shall)
SICK (vomit)	THIRSTY	WIN
SIGN / LANGUAGE	THIS	WINDOW
SILLY (daft)	THROUGH	WINTER
SING /ER	TIDY	WITH
SISTER	TIME	WOMAN
SIT / DOWN	TIRED	WON'T
SKIRT	TOAST (grill)	WORD
SKY (heaven)	TODAY	WORK
48 SLEEP	53 TOILET	58 WORSE
SLOW/LY	TOMATO	WRITE/R
SOCIAL WORKER	TOMORROW	WRONG
SOCK/S	TOP	YELLOW
SOME	TOWN	YES
SOON	TRAFFIC	YESTERDAY
SORRY	TRAIN (railway)	YOGHURT
SOUP / SPOON	TREE	YOU
SPEECH	TROUBLE	ZEBRA-CROSSING
49 SPOIL	54 TROUSERS	
SPOON	TRY	
SPRING (season)	UNDER	
STAND	UNTIL	
START	UP/STAIRS	
STAY	USE/FUL	
STOP (halt)	VERY	
STRONG	VOICE	
SUMMER	WAIT	
50 SUN/NY	55 WALK	
SUNDAY	WANT	
SWEET/S (toffee)	DON'T WANT	
SWIM/MING	WASH HANDS	
TABLE	WATCH ME	
TAKE	WE	
TALK	WEAR	
TAXI	LAST WEEK	
TEA (cuppa)	NEXT WEEK	